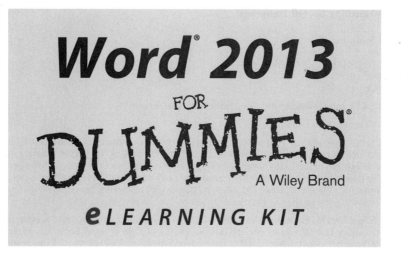

Word® 2013
FOR
DUMMIES®
A Wiley Brand

*e*LEARNING KIT

by Lois Lowe

FOR
DUMMIES®
A Wiley Brand

Word® 2013 eLearning Kit For Dummies®

Published by
John Wiley & Sons, Inc.,
111 River Street,
Hoboken,
NJ 07030-5774,
www.wiley.com

For general information on our other products and services, please contact our Customer Care Department within the U.S. at 877-762-2974, outside the U.S. at 317-572-3993, or fax 317-572-4002. For technical support, please visit www.wiley.com/techsupport.

Wiley publishes in a variety of print and electronic formats and by print-on-demand. Some material included with standard print versions of this book may not be included in e-books or in print-on-demand. If this book refers to media such as a CD or DVD that is not included in the version you purchased, you may download this material at http://booksupport.wiley.com. For more information about Wiley products, visit www.wiley.com.

Library of Congress Control Number: 2013957979

ISBN 978-1-118-49126-3 (pbk); ISBN 978-1-118-49190-4 (ebk); ISBN 978-1-118-49127-0 (ebk)

Manufactured in the United States of America

10 9 8 7 6 5 4 3 2 1

Contents at a Glance

Table of Contents

Introduction

*I*f you've been thinking about taking a class on the Internet (it is all the rage these days), but you're concerned about getting lost in the electronic fray, worry no longer. *Word 2013 eLearning Kit For Dummies* is here to help you, providing you with a hands-on learning experience that includes not only the book you hold in your hands, but also an online course at http://learn.dummies.com. Consider this introduction your primer.

About This Kit

Whether you follow along with the book, go online for the courses, or some combination of the two, the 11 chapters in *Word 2013 eLearning Kit For Dummies* walk you through examples and exercises so that you learn how to do the following:

- ✔ Master the basic features that all Office products have in common, like ribbons, scroll bars, and keyboard shortcuts.

- ✔ Create and format a basic Word document, whether you start from a blank document or one of the many templates.

- ✔ Save time and ensure document elements are formatted consistently by creating and customizing styles and templates.

- ✔ Apply different page-level settings in the same document by creating different sections within your document.

- ✔ Organize information into tables, and illustrate your content or simply decorate the page with graphics.

- ✔ Automate much of the work involved in handling correspondence and preparing long reports using Word's advanced document-preparation features.

- ✔ Protect and share documents using Word's security and sharing features.

Each piece of this kit works in conjunction with the others, although you don't need them all to gain valuable understanding of the key concepts.

This book uses a tutorial approach to explain how to use Word's features. In each chapter, you'll find the following elements:

- ✓ **Chapter opener questions:** To get you warmed up and ready for the chapter material, the questions quiz you on particular points of interest. If you don't know the answer, a page number heads you in the right direction to find it.

- ✓ **Tutorial step-by-step instruction with sample data files:** Each chapter introduces an important task you can do in Word. You then find step-by-step tutorials that walk you through using the feature or combining skills you've learned so far to accomplish a specific goal. Often, you need to download a sample file that goes with the steps. See the "Beyond the Book" section later in this introduction for details on downloading the sample files.

- ✓ **Summing Up:** This section appears at the end of each chapter; it briefly reiterates the content you just learned.

- ✓ **Try-it-yourself lab:** Test your knowledge of the content just covered by performing an activity *from scratch* — that is, using general steps only and no sample files.

- ✓ **Know this tech talk:** Each chapter contains a brief glossary of related terms.

A few style conventions help you navigate the book piece of this kit efficiently:

- ✓ Instructions and names of the files needed to follow along with the step lists are *italicized.*

- ✓ Website addresses, or URLs, are shown in a special typeface `like this`.

- ✓ Numbered steps that you need to follow and characters you need to type are set in **bold.**

Used in conjunction with the tutorial text, the online course that goes with this kit gives you the tools you need for a productive and self-guided eLearning experience. Here's how the course helps you get up-to-speed in Microsoft Word:

- ✓ **Multimedia-based instruction:** After each feature is introduced, you'll find plentiful video clips, illustrations, and interactive widgets that show you how a feature or task works. The course is like having a tutor ready and willing to show you how a process works as many times as you need until you're confident in what you've learned. Or if you're pretty comfortable with certain parts of Microsoft Word you can breeze past those parts of the course instead.

✔ **Interactive quizzes and activities:** Ample interactive elements enable you to understand how Microsoft Word works and check what you've learned. Hands-on activities enable you to try working in Word yourself and receive feedback on what skills you still need to practice.

✔ **Resources:** Throughout the online course, you'll find extra resources relevant to what you're learning.

Foolish Assumptions

For starters, I assume you need to find out how to use Word (and fast!) and want to get a piece of this academic action the fun and easy way with *Word 2013 eLearning Kit For Dummies.*

I assume you have basic Windows and computer skills, such as starting the computer and using the mouse.

To get the most out of this kit, you need a Windows computer running Word 2013. That way, you can experience the benefit of the tutorial steps in the book and the hands-on instruction in the online course.

Icons Used in This Kit

The familiar and helpful *For Dummies* icons point you in the direction of really great information that's sure to help you as you work your way through this kit. Look for these icons throughout the book and online course:

The Tip icon points out helpful information that's likely to make your job easier.

This icon marks an interesting and useful fact — something that you might want to remember for later.

The Warning icon highlights lurking danger. When you see this icon, you know to pay attention and proceed with caution.

Sometimes I might change things up by directing you to repeat a set of steps but with different parameters. If you're up for the challenge, look for the Practice icon.

Serving as your call to action, this icon sends you online to view web resources, to complete activities, or to find examples.

In addition to the icons, you also find two friendly study aids that bring your attention to certain pieces of information:

- **Lingo:** When you see the Lingo box, look for a definition of a key term or concept.
- **Extra Info:** This box highlights something to pay close attention to in a figure or points out other useful information that's related to the discussion.

Accessing the Word 2013 eCourse

Your purchase of this eLearning Kit includes access to the online eCourse. If you have purchased an electronic version of this book, please visit www. dummies.com/go/getelearningcode to gain your access code to the online course. If you purchased the paperback book, you find your access code inside the front cover this book.

Dummies eCourses require an HTML5-capable browser. If you use the Firefox or Chrome browser, make sure you have the latest version. Internet Explorer 11 is also HTML5-capable.

After you have your access code, go to http://learn.dummies.com to access the online course.

Beyond the Book

This section is your handy guide to finding all the content that goes with the book and eCourse, which includes the following:

- **Companion files:** You can download the companion files that go with the tutorial steps in this book online at www.dummies.com/go/word2013elearning.

✔ **Online articles and extras:** If you have questions about Word that you don't find answered in this kit, check out the free online articles at Dummies.com. You can also find help with evolving features that are related to Word, but that Microsoft is likely to change independently of Word, such as Microsoft's cloud storage space (that is, a free service for storing your files online so you can access them from anywhere).

Where to Go from Here

Now that you're primed and ready, time to begin.

Chapter 1
Getting to Know Word 2013

- ► Moving around in a document *enables you to view different parts of the document* that may not be onscreen at the moment. You can use scroll bars, arrow keys, and keyboard shortcuts in any combination.

- ► Changing the onscreen view *helps you focus on the important parts of the document* for the task you want to perform. Each application has its own unique set of views, as well as a Zoom control.

- ► Saving and opening documents *lets you store your work for later use* and then recall it to the screen when you're ready to continue. The Save As and Open dialog boxes share a common look and feel in all applications.

Microsoft Word is a word-processing application that can help you create many kinds of written documents, including reports, letters, newsletters, and labels. Word excels at any kind of text-based task.

Word is part of the Microsoft Office suite. A *suite* is a group of applications that are designed to work together and to have similar user interfaces that cut down on the learning curve for each one.

TIP

The time you spend now learning the Word interface will benefit you later if you decide to tackle any of the other Office applications.

Starting Word

The most straightforward way to start Word is to select it from the Windows 8 Start screen (or Windows 7 Start menu). You can browse through the list of programs, or you can start typing the application's name and then click its name when it appears.

Depending on how your PC is set up, you may also have a shortcut to Word on your desktop and/or on the taskbar.

TIP

You can double-click a data file that's associated with Word, but this method works only after you've created or saved a Word document on your computer.

When you're finished with Word, you can click its Close (X) button in its upper-right corner to exit. If you have any unsaved work, you're prompted to save it.

LINGO

Technically, a **program** can be any type of software, including Windows itself, whereas an **application** is a specific type of program that performs a useful user task, such as word processing.

Most nongeeky computer users don't recognize that distinction, though, and they use the terms interchangeably. So does this book.

Starting Word in Windows 8

In the following exercise, you practice opening and closing Word. This exercise is for Windows 8 users; if you have Windows 7, use the next exercise instead.

Files needed: None

1. **In Windows 8, press the Windows key to display the Start screen.**
2. **Click Word 2013. (Scroll to the right to locate that tile if needed, as in Figure 1-1.)**

   The Word application opens.
3. **Click the Close (X) button in the upper-right corner of the Word window.**

   The Word application window closes.
4. **Press the Windows key to reopen the Start screen.**
5. **Type Word.**

   The Search panel appears, and the Apps list is filtered to show only applications with "Word" in their names. See Figure 1-2.

Click the Word tile.

EXTRA INFO

If you don't see the Word application pinned to the Start screen, skip to Step 5 to use a different method of locating it.

Figure 1-1

Click Word 2013 in
the search results.

Windows suggests 2013.

Type Word here.

Figure 1-2

6. From the list of applications that appears, click Word 2013.

The Word application opens.

Leave Word open for the next exercise.

Figure 1-1 shows the Start screen for Windows 8.1, which allows you to create named groups for the tiles on the Start screen. In Figure 1-1, a group called Microsoft Office 2013 has been created, and shortcuts to each of the Office applications have been placed in that group. Your screen may look somewhat different depending on whether you have Windows 8.0 or Windows 8.1 and what groups have been created.

EXTRA INFO

If Word was not pinned to the Start screen in Step 2, before clicking on Word in Step 6 you can right-click it and choose Pin to Start to place a shortcut to Word on the Start screen for future use. You can also right-click it and choose Pin to Taskbar to place a shortcut for Word on the desktop's taskbar, so you don't have to return to the Start screen to start Word in the future.

Starting Word in Windows 7

In the following exercise, you practice opening and closing Word. This exercise is for Windows 7 users; if you have Windows 8, use the preceding exercise instead.

Files needed: None

1. **Click the Start button.**

   The Start menu opens.

2. **Click All Programs.**

   A list of all installed applications appears. Some of the applications are organized into folders.

3. **Click the Microsoft Office 2013 folder.**

   A list of the Microsoft Office 2013 applications appears.

4. **Click Word 2013.**

   The Word application opens.

5. **Click the Close (X) button in the upper-right corner of the Word window.**

   The Word application window closes.

6. **Click the Start button.**

7. **Type Word.**

   The Start menu is filtered to show applications that contain those letters in their names.

8. **From the list of applications that appears, click Word 2013.**

   The Word application opens.

Leave Word open for the next exercise.

Exploring the Word Interface

The Word 2013 interface consists of a tabbed Ribbon, a File menu, a status bar, window controls, and other common features. In the following sections, you become familiar with these common elements.

Exploring the Ribbon and tabs

All Office 2013 applications have a common system of navigation called the *Ribbon*, which is a tabbed bar across the top of the application window. Each tab is like a page of buttons. You click different tabs to access different sets of buttons and features.

New in Word 2013, a Start screen appears when you start the application. To bypass it and go to a new blank document, you can press Esc or click one of the templates that appears (such as Blank document).

In the following exercise, you practice using the commands on the Ribbon in Microsoft Word.

Files needed: None

Hover the mouse over Equation. . .

. . .to see its ScreenTip.

1. **If Word isn't already open from the preceding exercise, open it.**

2. **Press Esc or click Blank document to start a new document.**

3. **On the Ribbon, click the Insert tab.**

   Buttons for inserting various types of content appear.

   The buttons are organized into *groups;* the group names appear at the bottom. For example, the Pages group is the leftmost group.

4. **In the Symbols group, hover the mouse pointer over the Equation button.**

   A ScreenTip appears, telling you the button's name and purpose and showing a keyboard shortcut (Alt+=) that you can optionally use to select that command. See Figure 1-3.

5. **Click the Equation button.**

   A new equation box appears in the document, and the Equation Tools Design tab appears on the Ribbon. See Figure 1-4.

Figure 1-3

LINGO

The Equation Tools Design tab shown in Figure 1-4 is an example of a **contextual tab**. Contextual tabs appear only in certain contexts, such as when a particular type of object is active — in this case, an equation box.

Equation box

Figure 1-4

6. **Press Delete to remove the equation box.**

The Home tab reappears.

7. **Click the Insert tab again, and in the Header & Footer group, click the Header button.**

A menu opens. See Figure 1-5.

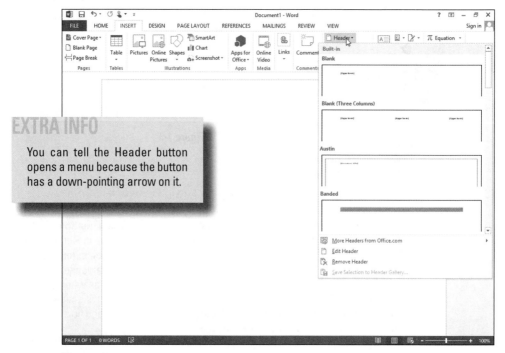

EXTRA INFO

You can tell the Header button opens a menu because the button has a down-pointing arrow on it.

Figure 1-5

8. **Click away from the menu to close it without making a selection.**

9. **In the Illustrations group, click SmartArt.**

    The Choose a SmartArt Graphic dialog box opens. See Figure 1-6.

Figure 1-6

10. **Click Cancel to close the dialog box without creating a graphic.**

11. **Click the Home tab, and in the Font group, click the Bold button.**

    The Bold attribute is toggled on. See Figure 1-7.

Bold button

Figure 1-7

12. **Type your first name.**

    Your first name appears in bold.

13. **Click the Bold button again.**

    The Bold attribute is toggled off.

14. **Press the space bar, and then type your last name.**

    Your last name does not appear in bold.

    In the Paragraph group, notice that the Align Left button is selected.

15. Click the Center button in the Paragraph group.

Your name is centered horizontally on the page. See Figure 1-8.

TIP

The paragraph alignment buttons are a set; when you select one, the previously selected button is deselected.

Center button

Centered text

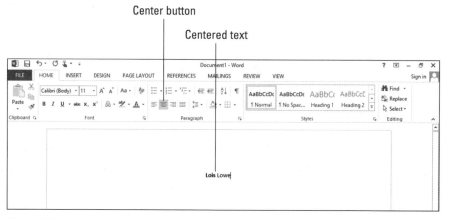

Figure 1-8

16. Click the Undo button on the Quick Access Toolbar.

See Figure 1-9. The last action is undone, and the paragraph alignment goes back to left alignment.

Undo button   Dialog box launcher for the Paragraph group

Figure 1-9

17. **Click the dialog box launcher button (shown in Figure 1-9) in the bottom-right corner of the Paragraph group.**

    A Paragraph dialog box opens. See Figure 1-10.

18. **Click Cancel to close the Paragraph dialog box.**

19. **If the Word window is maximized, click the Restore button in the upper-right corner so that the window is resizable.**

    See Figure 1-11.

20. **Note the buttons available in the Editing group on the Home tab.**

Figure 1-10

Restore button

Figure 1-11

21. **Drag the right border of the Word window toward the left, decreasing the size of the Word window until the Editing group collapses into a single large button.**

    See Figure 1-12.

Editing group collapsed

Figure 1-12

22. **Click the Editing button.**

    The menu that opens contains the buttons that were previously available from the Editing group. See Figure 1-13.

23. **Drag the right border of the Word window toward the right until the Editing group is expanded again. Click the Maximize button (second of the three buttons in the window's upper-right corner) if you want to maximize the window.**

Leave Word open for the next exercise.

Figure 1-13

Understanding the File menu

Clicking the File tab opens the File menu, also known as *Backstage view*. Backstage view provides access to commands that have to do with the data file you're working with — things like saving, opening, printing, mailing, and checking its properties. To leave Backstage view, click some other tab or press the Esc key.

In the following exercise, you practice using the File menu.

Files needed: None

1. **If Word isn't already open from the preceding exercise, open it, and then press Esc to display a new blank document.**

2. **Click the File tab on the Ribbon.**

   The File menu opens. Categories of commands are listed at the left.

The category that appears by default depends on whether any changes have been made to the blank document that opens by default when the application starts.

3. **Click Open if that category doesn't already appear by default.**

   This category provides shortcuts for reopening recently used files. See Figure 1-14.

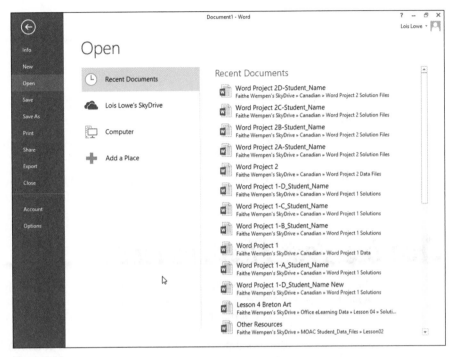

Figure 1-14

4. **Click the Info category and examine the commands available.**

   This category provides commands for permissions, sharing, and versions, as well as basic information about the file itself.

5. **Click the Manage Versions button.**

   This button opens a menu of additional commands. See Figure 1-15.

6. **Click away from the menu without choosing a command from it.**

   The menu closes.

7. **Click the New category.**

   Buttons appear for creating a new document based on a variety of templates.

8. **Click the Print category.**

   Buttons appear for printing the active document.

Figure 1-15

9. **Click the Share category.**

   Buttons appear for saving and distributing the active document in different formats.

10. **Click the Export category.**

    Options appear for getting help with the application.

11. **Click Close.**

    The active document and Backstage view close. If prompted to save your changes, click Don't Save. Word remains open.

12. **Close the Word Application by clicking the Close (X) button in the upper-right corner of the window.**

Creating Your First Document

When you start Word, a new blank document appears automatically, as you saw in the section "Starting Word." Just press Esc at Word's Start screen to access the new blank document. You can begin creating new content in this document and then save your work when you're finished. Alternatively, you can open an existing document or start a different type of document using one of Word's templates.

After starting a new document, you type or insert content into it. Documents can contain text, graphic objects, or a combination of the two. You can use many types of graphic objects, such as photos, clip art, drawings, diagrams, and charts. You learn about these object types in Chapter 8.

Starting a new blank document

In the following exercise, you start two new Word documents using different methods.

Files needed: None

1. **Start Microsoft Word 2013 using any method you like.**

   The Start screen appears. Icons for various template types appear. See Figure 1-16.

Figure 1-16

2. **Click Blank document.**

   A blank document appears.

3. **Press Ctrl+N to start another new blank document.**

   You can tell it is a different blank document because the name in the title bar changes.

4. **Choose File⇨Close to close one of the blank documents. Leave the other one open.**

Leave Word and the blank document open for the next exercise.

Typing text

You can type any text you like into a Word document, creating various document types from posters to dissertations. Just click in the large blank area in the center of the Word window and begin typing.

In the following exercise, you place text into a Word document.

Files needed: None

1. **If Word is not already open from the previous exercise, start Word and press Esc to access the new blank document.**

2. **Type** ACME Engineering, **press Enter to start a new paragraph, and then type** Making smart engineering decisions since 1962 **(see Figure 1-17).**

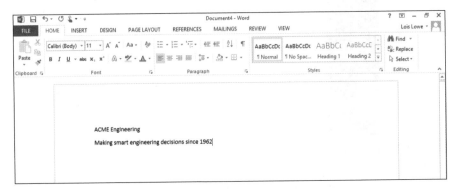

Figure 1-17

3. **Press Enter to move the insertion point to the next line, and then press the up-arrow key once to move the insertion point back into the text you typed.**

   The insertion point appears at the beginning of the word *Making.*

4. **Press the right-arrow key until the insertion point appears between 6 and 2 (see Figure 1-18), and then press the Backspace key to delete the 6.**

Insertion point

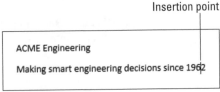

ACME Engineering

Making smart engineering decisions since 1962

Figure 1-18

If no text is selected, pressing Backspace removes the character to the *left* of the insertion point.

5. **Type** 7 **and then press the left-arrow key once.**

   The insertion point moves to the left of the 7.

6. **Press the Delete key to delete the 7.**

If no text is selected, pressing Delete removes the character to the *right* of the insertion point.

7. **Type** 6.

   The date once again appears as 1962.

Leave the document open for the next exercise.

The preceding steps walk you through the basics of typing text. In Chapter 2, you explore typing and editing text in more detail.

Inserting a picture

One of the most common graphic types is a *picture from file* (a picture that's saved as a separate file outside of Word). You can get pictures from the Internet, from friends, or from your own scanner or digital camera.

In the following exercise, you place a graphic into a Word document.

Files needed: 01Graphic01.jpg

1. **Start with the Word document open from the preceding exercise.**

LINGO

Word supports a wide variety of picture formats. Some of the most common formats include JPEG, TIF, GIF, BMP, and PNG. Those are **file extensions.** Most filenames include a period (.) followed by an extension, a code that indicates the file's type. Extensions are customarily three characters long, but do not have to be.

If you didn't do the preceding exercise, go back and complete it now.

2. **Click below the second paragraph to move the insertion point there.**

3. **Click the Insert tab on the Ribbon and click the Pictures button.**

   The Insert Picture dialog box opens.

4. **Navigate to the folder containing the data files for this chapter and select** 01Graphic01.jpg.

   See Figure 1-19.

Figure 1-19

5. Click the Insert button.

The picture is inserted in the document at the insertion point position.

The picture appears very large — larger than you might want it to be. Chapter 8 covers resizing a picture. In the meantime, you can drag a corner of the picture to resize it.

Leave the document open for the next exercise.

Saving and Opening Documents

Word can create, open, and save documents that contain the text, graphics, and other content you have entered into Word. If you don't save your work, whatever you've entered disappears when you close the application or turn off your computer.

Throughout the rest of this book, many of the exercises begin with an instruction to open a particular data file and end with an instruction to save it; when instructed to do those things, you can refer back to this section for help as needed.

Saving a document for the first time

As you work in Word, the content you create is stored in the computer's memory. This memory is only temporary storage. When you exit the application or shut down the computer, whatever is stored in memory is flushed away forever — unless you save it.

The first time you save a file, Word prompts you to enter a name for it in the Save As dialog box. You can also choose a different save location and/or file type.

When you resave an already saved file, the Save As dialog box doesn't reappear; the file saves with the most recent settings.

If you want to change the settings (such as the location or file type) or save under a different name, choose File⇨Save As to make the Save As dialog box appear.

Word saves its documents in a Word Document (.docx) format, by default, but it can also save in other formats for compatibility with other applications or for special uses. Two of the most common alternative file formats are

- **Macro-enabled files:** If you need to store macros in a Word document, you can save it in Word Macro-Enabled Document (.docm) format.

- **Word 97–2003:** Word includes a file format for backward compatibility with earlier versions of the application (versions 97 through 2003; the file format for Word 2007 and 2010 is identical to that of Word 2013, so you don't need a special format for backward compatibility with those versions). Some minor functionality may be lost when saving in the 97–2003 format. The file extension for it is .doc, and it does not have macro-enabled and non-macro-enabled variants; all are macro-enabled.

LINGO

Macros are recorded bits of code that can automate certain activities in a program. For example, a macro can record keystrokes for performing a task that needs to be repeated over and over, saving the user time. However, macros can also carry viruses. The default Word format doesn't support macros for that reason.

In this exercise, you save a document in Word several times with different names and file types.

Files needed: None

1. **Start in the document you created in the previous exercise, but have not saved yet.**

2. **Choose File⇨Save.**

   The Save As screen of Backstage view appears. Note that your SkyDrive is the default location selected under the Save As heading. In this exercise, however, you will save to your local computer.

3. **Click Computer.**

   A list of recently used folders on your local computer appears. See Figure 1-20.

4. **Click Browse.**

   The Save As dialog box opens, showing the default local location (probably your Documents library).

5. **In the File Name box, type** 01ACME.

   See Figure 1-21.

Figure 1-20

Figure 1-21

6. **Click Save.**

   The file is saved. The file's name appears in Word's title bar.

   Note: If you do not see the `.docx` extension, Windows may be set up to hide file extensions. That's okay; you don't need to see the file extensions here. If you want to see them anyway, in Windows 8 open a File Explorer window, and on the View tab, mark the File Name Extensions check box. Or, if you have Windows 7, from Windows Explorer open the Tools menu and choose Folder Options. In the dialog box that appears, click the View tab and clear the Hide Extensions for Known File Types check box.

7. **In the document, click the picture to select it, and then press the Delete key to remove it.**

8. **On the Quick Access Toolbar, click the Save button.**

   See Figure 1-22. The changes to the document are saved.

9. **In the document, drag across the words *ACME Engineering* to select those words, and then press Ctrl+B to bold them.**

10. **Press Ctrl+S.**

    The changes are saved.

11. **Drag across the last sentence to select it, and then press Ctrl+I to italicize it.**

Save button

Figure 1-22

12. **Choose File⇨Save As, and click the Browse button.**

    The Save As dialog box opens.

13. **In the File Name text box, change the filename to** 01ACME-Compatible.

14. **Click the drop-down list to the right of Save As Type.**

    A menu of document types opens.

15. **Select the Word 97–2003 Document option.**

    See Figure 1-23.

16. **Click Save.**

    The document is resaved with a different name and a different file type.

Leave the document open in Word for the next exercise.

Figure 1-23

Navigating in the Save and Open dialog boxes

Word 2013 uses the current Windows user's SkyDrive as the default storage location. SkyDrive is a cloud-based online storage area hosted by Microsoft. Anyone who registers for the service, or who logs into Windows 8 with a Microsoft ID, is given a certain amount of free storage space, and can purchase more. For more information about SkyDrive, see Appendix A.

You can also save your files locally, where the default location is your Documents library, as it was with Office 2010. In Windows, each user has his own Documents folder (based on who is logged into Windows at the moment).

New in Office 2013 applications, when you choose File➪Save As, a dialog box does not open immediately. Instead, a Save As screen in Backstage view opens, prompting you to choose an overall save location, either your SkyDrive or your Computer or some custom location you might have set up. Only after you make that choice does the Save As dialog box appear.

To understand how to change save locations, you should first understand the concept of a file path. Files are organized into folders, and you can have folders *inside* folders. For example, you might have

EXTRA INFO

If you want the Save As dialog box to appear immediately when you choose File➪Options, click Save, and mark the Don't Show the Backstage When Opening or Saving Files check box.

  ✔ A folder called *Work*

  ✔ Within that folder, another folder called *Job Search*

  ✔ Within that folder, a Word file called Resume.docx

The path for such a file would be

    C:\Work\Job Search\Resume.docx

When you change the save location, you're changing to a different path for the file. You do that by navigating through the file system via the Save As dialog box. The Save As dialog box provides several different ways of navigating, so you can pick the one you like best.

In this exercise, you experiment with several ways of changing the save location in the Save As dialog box.

Files needed: None

  1. **In Word, with the document still open from the previous exercise, choose File➪Save As.**

2. Click *Your Name*'s SkyDrive or Computer, depending on which location you want to save your work from the exercises in this book.

See Figure 1-24.

3. **Click Browse.**

The Save As dialog box opens.

4. **Change the Save As Type setting to Word Document (*.docx) if it is something different.**

5. **Change the filename to** 01ACME-Copy.

6. **Scroll through the navigation bar to see the available locations for saving files.**

See Figure 1-25.

7. **In the navigation bar, click This PC (if using Windows 8.1) or Computer (if using Windows 7 or 8.0).**

A list of drives appears. If you are using Windows 8, some folders may appear above the drives, so you may need to scroll down to see the drives.

Figure 1-24

Figure 1-25

8. **Double-click the C: drive.**

   A list of folders on the C: drive appears.

9. **Scroll in the navigation bar to locate the Documents shortcut and double-click it.**

   If you don't see a Documents shortcut, double-click This PC (in Windows 8.1) or Libraries (in Windows 7 and Windows 8.0) and Documents should appear below it.

   The Documents folder's content appears.

10. **Right-click an empty spot in right pane of the dialog box, point to New, and click Folder.**

    A new folder appears, with the name highlighted, ready for you to name it.

11. **Type** Dummies Kit **and press Enter to name the folder.**

    You've just created a folder that you can use to store all the work that you do for this eLearning Kit. See Figure 1-26.

New folder

Figure 1-26

12. **Double-click the Dummies Kit folder to open it.**

13. **In the Address bar, click the right-pointing arrow to the left of Dummies Kit.**

A list of all the other folders in the Documents folder appears.

In the Address bar, the parts of a path are separated by right-pointing tri-angles rather than by slashes. You can click any of the triangles to open a drop-down list containing all the *subfolders* (that is, the folders within that folder).

14. **Click any folder on that list to switch to that folder.**

15. **In the Address bar, click Documents.**

The Documents folder reappears.

16. **In the Address bar, click Libraries. Or, if Libraries does not appear (and it might not if you have Windows 8.1), click This PC.**

A list of libraries or default user folders appears: Documents, Pictures, Music, and Videos. See Figure 1-27.

Note: In Windows 8.1, libraries are available but not shown by default. To display the Libraries list in the navigation bar in Windows 8.1, right-click an empty area of the navigation bar and choose Show Libraries.

Figure 1-27

17. **In the navigation bar, click Desktop.**

    You can save directly to your desktop by saving to this location.

18. **In the navigation bar, click Documents and then double-click Dummies Kit.**

    The Dummies Kit folder reappears.

19. **In the File Name text box, type** Chapter 1 Practice.

    See Figure 1-28.

20. **Click Save.**

    A message appears that your document will be upgraded to the newest file format. This happens because, in an earlier exercise, you saved this file in Word 97-2003 format, and it is still in that format.

Figure 1-28

21. **Click OK to save the file.**

22. **Choose File⇨Close to close the document without exiting Word.**

Opening a document

When you open a file, you copy it from your hard drive (or other storage location) into the computer's memory, where Word can access it for viewing and modifying it.

The Open dialog box's navigation controls are almost exactly the same as those in the Save As dialog box, so you can browse to a different storage location if needed.

If you want to reopen a recently used file, there's an even quicker way than using the Open dialog box. Choose File⇨Open and then click the file's name on the Recent Files list.

In this exercise, you open a saved file.

Files needed: Any saved Word document, such as the Chapter 1 Practice file you save in the previous exercise

1. **In Word, choose File⇨Open.**

2. **Click either *Your Name* SkyDrive or Computer, depending on where you chose to save in the previous exercise.**

3. **Click Browse.**

   The Open dialog box appears. The location shown is the Dummies Kit folder because it was the last folder you accessed during this session.

4. **Click Chapter 1 Practice.**

   See Figure 1-29.

Figure 1-29

5. **Click Open.**

   The file opens in Word.

6. **Choose File⇨Close to close the document without exiting Word.**

7. **Choose File⇨Open.**

   A list of recently opened files appears on the right side of the screen.

8. **Click Chapter 1 Practice.**

   That file reopens.

9. **Choose File➪Close to close the document again.**

Recovering lost work

Computers lock up occasionally, and applications crash in the middle of important projects. When that happens, any work that you haven't saved is gone.

To minimize the pain of those situations, Word has an AutoRecover feature that silently saves your drafts as you work, once every ten minutes or at some other interval you specify. These drafts are saved in temporary hidden files that are deleted when you close the application successfully (that is, not abruptly because of a lockup, crash, or power outage). If the application crashes, those temporary saved files appear for your perusal when the program restarts. You can choose to do either of the following:

✔ Save them if their versions are newer than the ones you have on your hard drive.

✔ Discard them if they contain nothing you need.

In this exercise, you change the interval at which Word saves backup drafts for AutoRecover.

Files needed: None

1. **In Word, choose File➪Options.**

   The Word Options dialog box opens.

2. **Click the Save category on the left.**

3. **Make sure that the Save AutoRecover Information Every xx Minutes check box is selected.**

4. **If desired, change the value in the Minutes box to another number.**

   For example, to save every five minutes, type **5** there. See Figure 1-30.

5. **Click OK.**

Leave Word open for the next exercise.

Set the AutoRecover interval.

Figure 1-30

Moving Around

As you work in Word, you may add so much content that you can't see it all onscreen at once. You might need to scroll through the document to view different parts of it. The simplest way to scroll through a document is by using the scroll bars with your mouse.

Scrolling through a document with the scroll bars doesn't move the insertion point, so what you type or insert doesn't necessarily appear in the location that shows onscreen.

You can also get around by moving the insertion point. When you do so, the document view scrolls automatically so you can see the newly selected location. You can move the insertion point either by clicking where you want it or by using keyboard shortcuts.

Moving with the mouse

Here's a summary of the available mouse movements:

- ✔ Click a scroll arrow to scroll a small amount in that direction.
- ✔ Click above or below the scroll box to scroll one full screen in that direction if the document is tall/wide enough that there's undisplayed content in that direction.
- ✔ Drag the scroll box to scroll quickly in the direction you're dragging.

Now practice these skills in the following exercise.

In the following exercise, you move around in a Word document via the mouse.

Files needed: Chapter 1 Syllabus.docx

Bottom scroll arrow
on vertical scroll bar

1. **In Word, open Chapter 1 Syllabus and save it as Chapter 1 Syllabus Practice.**

2. **Click the bottom scroll arrow on the vertical scroll bar three times.**

   Each time you click, the display scrolls down a small amount. See Figure 1-31.

Figure 1-31

3. **Click once below the scroll box.**

   The display scrolls down one screenful.

4. **Drag the scroll box up as high as it will go.**

   The top of the document comes back into view.

5. **Click and hold down the mouse button on the top scroll arrow.**

   The bottom of the document comes into view.

Leave the document open for the next exercise.

> **EXTRA INFO**
>
> The size of the scroll box is an indicator of how much of the document is undisplayed at the moment.

Moving with the keyboard

Here's a summary of the ways you can move around in a document via the keyboard:

- ✔ Press an arrow key to move the insertion point in the direction of the arrow. The up- and down-arrow keys move one line, and the right- and left-arrow keys move one character.

↙ Press the Page Up or Page Down key to scroll one full screen in that direction.

↙ Press the Home key to move to the left side of the current line.

↙ Press the End key to move to the right side of the current line.

↙ Press Ctrl+Home to move to the beginning of the document.

↙ Press Ctrl+End to move to the end of the document.

Now practice those skills in the following exercise.

In the following exercise, you move around in a Word document via the keyboard.

Files needed: Chapter 1 Syllabus Practice.docx, open from the preceding exercise

1. **In Chapter 1 Syllabus Practice, press Ctrl+Home.**

   The insertion point moves to the beginning of the document.

2. **Press the right-arrow key on the keyboard twice.**

   The insertion point moves two spaces to the right.

3. **Press the down-arrow key twice.**

   The insertion point moves two lines down so that it is in the Description paragraph. See Figure 1-32.

Insertion point

CIT 233
Computer Hardware/Software Architecture
Description
This course presents a detailed investigation of computer hardware and software. Looking at hardware and software components along with several operating systems, students should enhance their knowledge of the interrelations between these components. In addition, through the use of programming examples, the student will learn about the structure of the microprocessor and microcomputer basics and gain detailed knowledge of computer components and their functions. By the end of the course, students will be able to identify, describe, and discuss the concepts of computer structure, architecture, and performance. Students will also apply knowledge gained in discussing and solving problem-based scenarios.

Figure 1-32

4. **Hold down the Ctrl key and press the down-arrow key.**

   The insertion point moves to the beginning of the next paragraph.

5. **Hold down the Ctrl key and press the right-arrow key.**

   The insertion point moves to the next word in the paragraph.

6. **Press the Home key.**

   The cell cursor moves back to the beginning of the paragraph.

7. **Press the Page Down key.**

   The page scrolls down one screenful. (The exact amount depends on your screen size.)

8. **Press Ctrl+Home.**

   The cell cursor moves back to the top of the document.

Leave the document open for the next exercise.

Changing the Onscreen View

Word has multiple viewing modes you can switch among to make it easier to do different kinds of writing and editing. For example, Word's Outline view is optimal for creating outlines, and Full Screen Reading view works well for reading long documents on a computer monitor.

In addition, Word has Zoom commands that can make the text and graphics appear larger or smaller onscreen while you work.

Zooming has no relationship to the size of the text or graphics when they print; it affects only the onscreen view.

Changing views

The default view in Word is Print Layout; it displays a document very similarly to the way it will print, including all graphics, multicolumn layouts, and page breaks.

The alternatives to Print Layout view are

- ✔ **Read Mode:** A view designed to optimize readability onscreen.
- ✔ **Web Layout:** A view designed to mimic web content; use this view to see how your document might look if saved in web format.
- ✔ **Outline:** A hierarchical view in which each heading level is a level in an outline, and body text can optionally be hidden.
- ✔ **Draft:** A simple text-only view that hides most graphics and ignores multi-column layouts and page headers and footers.

In this exercise, you explore the available views in Word.

Files needed: Chapter 1 Syllabus Practice.docx, open from the preceding exercise

1. In Chapter 1 Syllabus Practice, click the View tab.

Buttons for each of the available views appear on the Ribbon. See Figure 1-33.

Figure 1-33

2. Choose View⇨Read Mode.

The display changes to show the document in an easy-to-read layout. See Figure 1-34.

Menu bar

Figure 1-34

3. **Click the View command on the menu bar at the top of the screen and click Edit Document on the menu that appears to return to normal viewing.**

4. **Choose View⇨Web Layout.**

   The display changes to show the document in a margin-less layout that resembles a web page.

5. **Choose View⇨Draft.**

   The display changes to show the document in Draft view.

6. **Scroll through the document in Draft view.**

EXTRA INFO

Draft view shows the text in a very basic format, without multiple columns, headers/footers, or other layout elements.

REMEMBER

Page breaks are indicated by dotted lines, as shown in Figure 1-35.

Page break line

Figure 1-35

7. Choose View➪Outline.

The display changes to show the document in Outline view. An Outlining tab appears on the Ribbon. This document doesn't outline very well because no headings have been set up in this document yet.

8. Choose Outlining➪Close Outline View.

The display returns to Print Layout view.

9. Hover the mouse over the Web Layout button on the status bar.

The status bar is the blue bar at the bottom of the Word window. A ScreenTip appears indicating it is the Web Layout button. See Figure 1-36.

10. Hover the mouse over each of the other view buttons on the status bar to see their names.

Leave Word open for the next exercise.

Figure 1-36

EXTRA INFO

Several of the views have an equivalent button on the status bar for quick view changes, so you don't have to open the View tab each time you want to change the view.

Zooming in and out

Zooming changes the magnification of the data shown onscreen. Zooming doesn't change the magnification of the application window itself (for example, the Ribbon), and it doesn't change the size of the data on printouts.

Zooming in increases the magnification, and zooming out decreases it.

In this exercise, you explore the Zoom feature in Word.

Files needed: Chapter 1 Syllabus Practice.docx, open from the preceding exercise

1. In Chapter 1 Syllabus Practice, drag the Zoom slider all the way to the right.

The Zoom slider is located in the bottom-right corner of the Word window. The zoom level increases to 500 percent. See Figure 1-37.

Zoom slider

Figure 1-37

2. **Drag the Zoom slider to the left, so that the zoom setting is 50%.**

When the zoom magnification decreases to 50%, the document's two pages appear side by side.

3. **Click the plus sign at the right end of the Zoom slider.**

The zoom increases slightly.

4. **Click the minus sign at the left end of the Zoom slider.**

The zoom decreases slightly.

5. **Click the current zoom percentage (the number to the right of the Zoom slider).**

The Zoom dialog box opens. See Figure 1-38.

Figure 1-38

 You can also open the Zoom dialog box by clicking the View tab on the Ribbon and clicking the Zoom button.

6. **In the Zoom dialog box, select 100% and then click OK.**

The zoom changes back to 100 percent (the default).

7. **Close the document. Do not save changes if prompted.**

Exit Word.

 # Summing Up

In this chapter, you explored the Word interface. You learned how to start and exit Word, move around in a document, create and save your work, and adjust the view.

- ✔ The Ribbon File tab takes you to Backstage view, where you can manage files.

- ✔ Word starts a new, blank document when it opens, and displays a Start screen on top of it. You can bypass the Start screen and access the new blank document by pressing Esc.

✔ To enter text in a document, click where you want to place the text; doing so moves the insertion point to the place where you click. Then type.

✔ To insert a picture, click the Insert tab on the Ribbon and then click the Picture button.

✔ Scroll bars enable you to scroll to different parts of a document. You can also move around by clicking where you want to go or by using the arrow keys to move the insertion point.

✔ To save your work, choose File⇨Save, press Ctrl+S, or click the Save button on the Quick Access Toolbar.

✔ To open a file, choose File⇨Open. You can also select a recently used file from the Recent section of the File menu's Open category.

✔ You can switch among views on the View tab.

✔ The Zoom feature increases or decreases the magnification of the data displayed onscreen. Use the Zoom slider and controls in the lower-right corner of the application window.

Try-it-yourself lab

For more practice with the features covered in this chapter, try the following exercise on your own:

1. **Start Word and, in the new document that appears, type** Grocery List**.**

2. **Press Enter to start a new paragraph and then type a grocery shopping list of at least six items, pressing Enter after each one.**

3. **Save the file as** Chapter 1 Grocery List **in the Dummies Kit folder you created earlier and close Word.**

Know this tech talk

application: A program that performs a useful user task, such as creating a word-processing document or calculating a number.

Backstage view: The section of Word that appears when the File menu is open. It contains commands for working with files, setting program options, importing, exporting, and printing.

document: A data file in a word-processing program. Can also refer generically to any data file.

file extension: The code following the period at the end of a filename, indicating the file's type.

folder: An organizing container on a hard drive in which to store files.

insertion point: A flashing vertical line indicating where text will be inserted when you type.

scroll bar: A bar along the right and/or bottom side of a window that can be used to change the viewing area.

scroll box: The movable box inside the scroll bar.

Chapter 2

Creating a Word Document

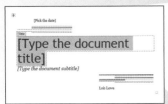

✔ Starting new documents based on templates can *save time and provide guidance as to what content to insert and where to place it.* Many templates are available for free via Office.com.

✔ Selecting text before issuing a command *enables you to act on large blocks of text at a time.* You can select text with either the keyboard or the mouse.

✔ Finding and replacing text *makes editing easier.* You can identify all instances of a particular word or phrase and replace them with a different word or phrase.

✔ Check your spelling and grammar to *avoid embarrassing errors* in documents you distribute to others. Word can help you check individual words and the entire document easily.

✔ You can *share your documents with other people* via e-mail or by printing them. You can begin sending a document via e-mail from within Word, and your default e-mail program opens to send the message.

Microsoft Word is the most popular Office application because nearly everyone needs to create text documents of one type or another. With Word, you can create everything from cover sheets to school research papers to family holiday letters.

In this chapter, I explain how to create, edit, proofread, and share simple documents. By the end of this chapter, you have a good grasp of the entire process of creating documents, from start to finish, including how to share your work with others via print or e-mail. Later chapters then build on this knowledge, adding in the fancier aspects, such as using formatting, styles, graphics, and multiple sections.

Starting a New Word Document

As you learn in Chapter 1, you can create a blank new document or you can base a new document on a template. Word 2013 uses templates stored on Office.com, and you can access that site directly from within Word, as long as your computer is connected to the Internet. After starting a new document, you can adjust the paper size and orientation if needed.

LINGO

A **template** is a special type of document that's designed to be a model for new documents. Templates have a different file extension than regular documents (either `.dotx` or `.dotm`). When you start a new document based on a template, the template file itself is unaffected, so the template is always the same each time you use it.

REMEMBER

Even when you start a blank document, you still (technically) use a template. The blank document uses a Normal template, and it specifies certain default settings for a new blank document, such as the default fonts (Calibri for body text and Cambria for headings), default font sizes (11 point for body text), and margins (1 inch on all sides).

EXTRA INFO

When you create a new document by clicking the Blank Document icon or by pressing Ctrl+N, the resulting document is based on the Normal template. If you stick with the default values for the Normal template's definition, the Normal template doesn't exist as a separate file; it's built into Word itself. You won't find the template if you search your hard drive for it. However, if you make a change to one or more of the Normal template's settings, Word saves them to a Normal.dotm file. If Word at any point can't find Normal.dotm, it reverts to its internally stored copy and goes back to the default values.

That's important to know because if you ever accidentally redefine the Normal template so that it produces documents with unwanted settings or if it ever gets corrupted, all you have to do is find and delete Normal.dotm from your hard drive, and you go back to a fresh-from-the-factory version of the default settings for new, blank documents. The template is stored in C:\Users\user\AppData\Roaming\Microsoft\Templates, in which *user* is the logged-in username.

Creating a new document using a template

You can easily create a new document based on a template. This new document has all the characteristics of the template, including margins, paper size, default fonts, and any sample content that the template contains.

In the following exercise, you start two new Word documents. One uses a local template, and one uses a template from Office.com.

Files needed: None

1. **In Word, choose File⇨New.**

   Thumbnails of templates for creating new documents appear, as shown in Figure 2-1.

2. **In the Search for Online Templates box, type** Brochures **and press Enter.**

   Word uses your Internet connection to retrieve a list of available brochure templates.

3. **Scroll down and click the Brochure for Small Business template.**

   A preview of it appears. See Figure 2-2.

Figure 2-1

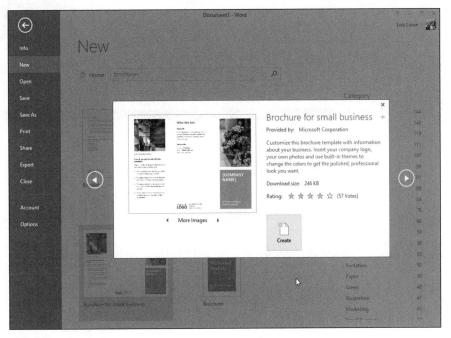

Figure 2-2

4. Click the Create button.

The template is downloaded, and a new document appears based on it. See Figure 2-3.

5. Examine the document to see what types of content the template provides, choose File⇨Close to close the document, and if prompted to save your changes, click Don't Save.

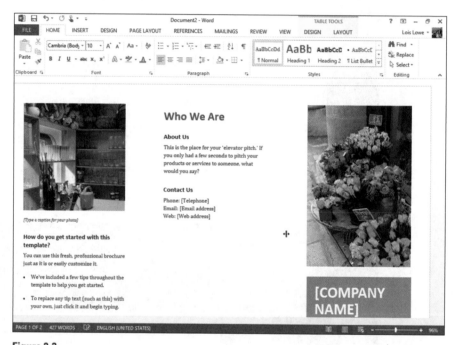

Figure 2-3

6. Choose File⇨New.

The icons reappear for new document types.

7. In the Search for Online Templates box, type Urban Report **and press Enter.**

A list of the templates matching that name appears.

8. Click Report (Urban theme).

A sample of the template appears. See Figure 2-4.

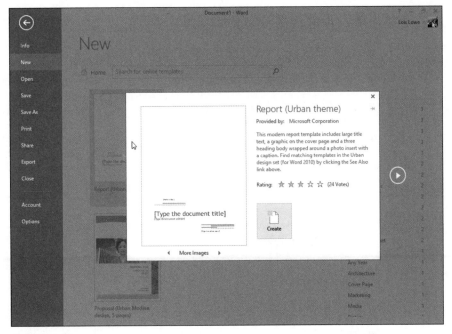

Figure 2-4

9. **Click the Create button.**

   A new document opens based on the selected template.

10. **Scroll through the new document and notice the placeholders ready for you to fill in to create your own version of the report.**

11. **Save the document as *Chapter 2 Practice*.**

    If you see a message about upgrading the document to the newest file format, click OK.

Leave the document open for the next exercise.

PRACTICE

For more practice, create several more new documents by using different templates. Don't save any of them.

Setting page margins

Word provides several easy-to-use presets. You can also individually specify the margins for each side of the page if you prefer.

In the following exercise, you change the page margins in two ways: using a preset and using an exact value.

Files needed: Chapter 2 Practice, open from the preceding exercise

1. **In the Chapter 2 Practice document, choose Page Layout⇨Margins⇨Narrow (see Figure 2-5).**

   Presets for narrow margins are applied to the top, bottom, right, and left margins for the document.

Figure 2-5

2. Click the Margins button again, and then choose Custom Margins.

The Page Setup dialog box opens.

3. In the Top, Bottom, Left, and Right boxes, type 1.3, **as shown in Figure 2-6, and then click OK.**

The margins change.

You can tell because the sample text is positioned differently on the pages.

4. Save your work.

Leave the document open for the next exercise.

Figure 2-6

Setting page size and orientation

A template might not always use the right paper size or page orientation for the work you want to create. In some cases, either or both may require adjustment.

The standard paper size in the U.S. is 8.5 x 11 inches, also known as Letter. Most of the templates available through Word use this paper size, although some exceptions exist. For example, an Envelopes template might use a page size that matches a standard business envelope, or a legal brief template might use legal-size paper (8.5 x 14 inches).

In the following exercise, you set the page orientation of a document to Landscape and change its paper size.

Files needed: Chapter 2 Practice, open from the preceding exercise

1. In the Chapter 2 Practice document, choose Page Layout➪Orientation➪Landscape (see Figure 2-7).

The page changes to Landscape mode.

LINGO

A document's **orientation** can be in either Portrait or Landscape mode. **Portrait** is a standard page in which the long side of the paper runs along the left and right. **Landscape** is a rotated page in which the long side of the paper runs along the top and bottom.

2. **Click the Orientation button and choose Portrait to change the orientation back to Portrait mode.**

3. **Click the Size button, and in the drop-down list that appears (see Figure 2-8), choose A4 8.27" x 11.69".**

   You may need to scroll down to find this option. The options available on the menu may be different from the ones shown here, or in a different order.

   The paper size changes.

Figure 2-7

Changing the paper size in Word doesn't change the paper size in your printer, of course, so if you print on a different sized paper than you tell Word you're using, the printing may not be centered on the paper.

For more practice, click the Size button, choose More Paper Sizes, and set up a custom paper size by entering a width and height on the Paper tab of the Page Setup dialog box.

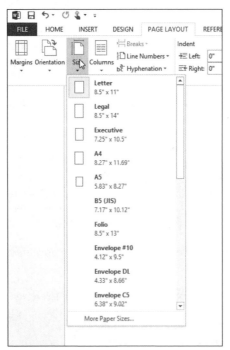

Figure 2-8

EXTRA INFO

A4 is a commonly used paper size in Europe. Look online for websites that explain the paper sizes common in various countries. Here's one such site: `www.cl.cam.ac.uk/~mgk25/iso-paper.html`.

4. **Save your work.**

Leave the document open for the next exercise.

Editing Text

After creating a document and setting its basic properties, such as margins, orientation, and page size, you're ready to edit its content. Editing can include adding text, deleting text, modifying text, and moving and copying blocks of text from one location to another.

If you used a template to get started, you may already have some sample content in the document (text and/or graphics). You can edit this content, or you can delete it and start from scratch.

Filling text placeholders

Some templates include placeholders to guide you in creating content in a specific format. You aren't required to use the placeholders; you can delete them if you like. However, if you aren't sure how to get started with a particular type of document, the template's placeholders can be helpful guides.

In the following exercise, you edit a document's text by filling in placeholders.

Files needed: Chapter 2 Practice, open from the preceding exercise

1. **In the Chapter 2 Practice document, click in the *[Type the document title]* placeholder on the first page.**

The placeholder becomes highlighted. See Figure 2-9.

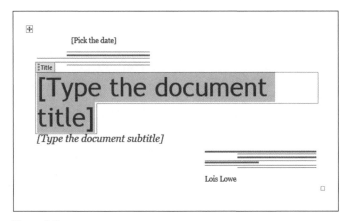

[Pick the date]

Title

[Type the document title]

[Type the document subtitle]

Lois Lowe

Figure 2-9

2. **Type** Mountain Vista Vacations.

   The text appears in the placeholder box.

3. **Click in the *[Type the document subtitle]* placeholder and type** Affordable Family Fun.

4. **Click in the *[Pick the date]* placeholder.**

   The text becomes highlighted, and a drop-down arrow appears to its right.

5. **Click the arrow to open a date picker (see Figure 2-10), click the Today button to select today's date, and click the name that appears in the document.**

   By default, the name that appears is the name of the registered user of this copy of Word.

6. **If it's not your name that appears already, type your own name.**

Figure 2-10

The cover page information is now complete, as shown in Figure 2-11.

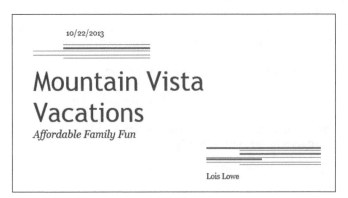

Figure 2-11

7. **Save your work and close the document.**

Leave Word open for the next exercise.

Typing and editing text

Most documents don't contain text placeholders, so you're on your own in deciding what to type. Fortunately, you can easily type and edit text in Word.

When you type in Word, the insertion point automatically moves to the next line when you run out of room at the right margin. You don't have to press Enter to break each line manually. The only time you need to press Enter is when you want to start a new paragraph.

You can press the Delete key to delete text to the right of the insertion point, or press the Backspace key to delete text to the left of the insertion point. To delete more than one character at once, select the block of text to delete, and then press either Delete or Backspace.

You can also select some text and then type over it. When you type after selecting text, the selected text is replaced by what you type.

In the following exercise, you type some text in a new document and then edit it using several editing techniques.

Files needed: None

1. **In Word, press Ctrl+N to start a new blank document.**

2. **Type the following text in the document:**

   Dear Karen:

   Florida is certainly a long way from home, and although we are enjoying our trip, we're looking forward to being home again with our good friends.

   We're having a wonderful time on our vacation. The weather has been perfect. Elroy and George have been collecting shells, and Judy and I have been enjoying the pool.

3. **Triple-click the last paragraph to select it.**

4. **Click and drag the paragraph up, and then drop it between the other two paragraphs (right below the salutation). See Figure 2-12.**

Figure 2-12

5. **Double-click the name *Karen* in the first paragraph and type** Rosie.

6. **Click to move the insertion point after the word *Florida* in the last paragraph. Press the Backspace key until the entire word is deleted, and then type** California.

7. **Use the arrow keys to move the insertion point before *shells* in the second body paragraph of the letter, and then type** sea.

The document resembles Figure 2-13.

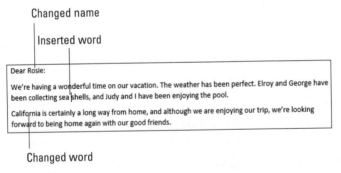

Figure 2-13

8. **Save the document as *Chapter 2 Vacation*.**

Leave the document open for the next exercise.

Adding symbols and special characters

Word enables you add pretty much any character or symbol you might need, such an accent over a vowel, a special punctuation mark, a currency symbol, and much more. *¿Cómo, señorita?*

To find these characters, open the Insert tab and choose Symbol⇨More Symbols.

In the Symbol dialog box, here's how to find different types of characters or symbols:

- **Characters specific to your current font:** If you want the character or symbol to match your document's font, make sure the Symbols tab is open. Then choose your desired font from the Font drop-down list and browse through the characters that are included with that font.

- **Characters that are pictures:** Again on the Symbols tab, choose the Wingdings font or another picture font to find a wide selection of characters that look like pictures.

- **Special punctuation and legal symbols:** On the Special Characters tab, you find options for inserting em dashes and en dashes as well as legal symbols such as a copyright symbol or registered trademark symbol.

Selecting Text

Selecting blocks of text before you issue an editing or formatting command allows you to act on the entire block at once. For example, you can select multiple paragraphs before applying new line spacing or indentation settings, and those settings apply to every paragraph in the selection.

You have many ways to select text:

- Click and drag across the text with the left mouse button pressed to select any amount of text.

- Move the insertion point to the beginning of the text, and then hold down the Shift key while you press the arrow keys to extend the selection.

- Press the F8 key to turn on Extend mode, and then you can use the arrow keys to extend the selection.

- Double-click a word to select it or triple-click a paragraph to select it.

- Press Ctrl+A to select the entire document.

- Click to the left of a line to select that line.

In the following exercise, you practice selecting parts of a document.

Files needed: Chapter 2 Vacation, open from the preceding exercise

1. **In the Chapter 2 Vacation file, triple-click the middle paragraph to select it.**

2. **Hold down the Shift key and press the down-arrow key twice to extend the selection to the next paragraph (see Figure 2-14).**

PRACTICE

For more practice, click away from the selected paragraphs to deselect them. Then double-click several words to select them. Next, double-click one word and hold down the Shift key while you double-click a different word. Try it again with the Ctrl key instead of Shift.

Dear Rosie:

We're having a wonderful time on our vacation. The weather has been perfect. Elroy and George have been collecting sea shells, and Judy and I have been enjoying the pool.

California is certainly a long way from home, and although we are enjoying our trip, we're looking forward to being home again with our good friends.

Figure 2-14

3. **Press Ctrl+A to select the entire document, and then click away from the selected text to deselect it.**

4. **Drag the mouse across the word *wonderful* to select it, and then position the mouse pointer to the left of the first line in the second paragraph.**

   The mouse pointer turns into a white arrow that points diagonally up and to the right.

REMEMBER

If you don't see the arrow, make sure you are in Print Layout view. On the View tab, click Print Layout.

5. **Click to select the line (see Figure 2-15).**

We're having a wonderful time on our vacation. The weather has been perfect. Elroy and George have been collecting sea shells, and Judy and I have been enjoying the pool.

California is certainly a long way from home, and although we are enjoying our trip, we're looking forward to being home again with our good friends.

Figure 2-15

6. **Close the document without saving your changes because you didn't make any in this exercise.**

Leave Word open for the next exercise.

Manipulating Text

You can manually move around in a document making edits and rearranging text, but it is often more efficient to use the tools in Word that are especially designed for helping you find, replace, and sort text.

In the following sections, you learn about the Find pane in Word and how to use it to quickly find all instances of a text string. You also learn how to replace one text string with another and how to sort a list of items alphabetically without manually rearranging them.

Finding text

The Navigation pane in Word serves several purposes. One of these is to display the results of a search for a text string you enter. You can open the Navigation pane by pressing Ctrl+F or by selecting the Navigation Pane check box on the View tab. In the Navigation pane, you can enter the text string you want to find in the Search Document box at the top. A list of all the instances of that text string appears in the Navigation pane. To jump to any instance, click it in the pane.

In the following exercise, you use the Find feature to find instances of some text.

Files needed: Chapter 2 Letter.docx

1. **In Word, open the Chapter 2 Letter file and save it as Chapter 2 Letter Practice.**

2. **Choose Home⇨Find or press Ctrl+F, the keyboard shortcut for Find.**

   The Navigation pane opens with the Results tab displayed.

3. **In the text box at the top of the Navigation pane, type** King **and press Enter.**

   Both instances of King are highlighted in the letter. The first instance is selected in the document. See Figure 2-16.

EXTRA INFO

In Word 2007 and earlier, a Find dialog box opened when you pressed Ctrl+F, enabling you to search through the document via a dialog box interface. That interface is still available, but you have to work a little harder to get to it now. From the Navigation pane, click the down arrow to the right of the Search Document box and choose Advanced Find from the menu that appears. The Find and Replace dialog box appears. This is the same dialog box, by the way, that you use when you replace text (which I cover in the next section). The keyboard shortcut for the Replace command is Ctrl+H, so one quick way to get to the Find feature in the Find and Replace dialog box is to press Ctrl+H and then click the Find tab.

First instance is selected and highlighted.

Other instance is highlighted.

Figure 2-16

4. **In the Navigation pane, click the second instance.**

   The second instance is selected in the document.

5. **In the text box at the top of the Navigation pane, select King, type** Sycamore Industries, **and press Enter.**

   Four instances of Sycamore Industries are highlighted in the document.

6. **In the Navigation pane, click each of the instances to jump to it in the document.**

7. **Click the Close (X) button in the upper-right corner of the Navigation pane to close it.**

Leave the document open for the next exercise.

Replacing text

Not only can you find specific text in a document, but you can also replace it with other text. This can be helpful, for example, if a company or person changes his or her name and you need to make a report or letter reflect that.

You can change individual instances one-by-one, or you can use the Replace All feature to replace all instances at once.

Replace All is very convenient, but be careful that you don't make unintended changes with it; sometimes a text string you replace is part of another word or phrase that shouldn't be changed.

In the following exercise, you use the Replace feature to change the name of a company in a letter.

Files needed: Chapter 2 Letter Practice.docx, open from the preceding exercise

1. **In Chapter 2 Letter Practice, press Ctrl+Home to move the insertion point to the top of the document.**

2. **Choose Home⇨Replace.**

   The Find and Replace dialog box opens with the Replace tab displayed.

Ctrl+H is the keyboard shortcut for Replace.

3. **In the Find What box, type** Sycamore Industries **and in the Replace With box, type** Dumont Fabrication **(see Figure 2-17).**

4. **Click the Find Next button.**

   The first instance of Sycamore Industries appears highlighted in the document.

Figure 2-17

TIP You can drag the title bar of the Find and Replace dialog box to move the dialog box out of the way if it obscures the found text.

5. **Click the Replace button to replace the first instance.**

6. **Click the More button to reveal additional options, and then select the Match Case check box.**

   The operation is restricted to instances that match the Find What text string's capitalization. See Figure 2-18.

7. **Click the Replace All button.**

   All remaining instances that match in capitalization are replaced. A dialog box appears stating that Word has reached the end of the document and three replacements were made.

8. **Click OK to close the message box.**

Figure 2-18

9. **Click the Close button to close the Find and Replace dialog box, and then save the document by pressing Ctrl+S.**

Leave the document open for the next exercise.

Sorting a list

As you type a list of items, it might not occur to you that you want them sorted into alphabetical order. Never fear, though — it's easy to sort a list alphabetically in Word. Word sorts by the first letter of each paragraph, so each item in the list must be a separate paragraph.

In the following exercise, you use the Sort feature to reorder a list.

LINGO

Sorts can be **ascending,** which means A to Z, or **descending,** which means Z to A. In an ascending sort, numbers and symbols come before letters; in a descending sort, they come after letters.

Files needed: Chapter 2 Letter Practice.docx, open from the preceding exercise

1. **In Chapter 2 Letter Practice, select the bulleted list.**

   To do so, click and drag the mouse pointer across the entire bulleted list.

2. **Choose Home⇨Sort, and in the Sort Text dialog box that opens (see Figure 2-19), click OK.**

   The Sort button has an A-Z icon and is in the Paragraph group.

   The list is sorted in ascending order. See Figure 2-20.

3. **Save and close the document.**

Leave Word open for the next exercise.

Figure 2-19

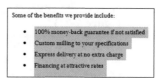

Figure 2-20

Checking Spelling and Grammar

Spelling and grammar errors in your documents can leave a bad impression with your audience and cause lost customers, jobs, and opportunities. Fortunately, Word can help you find and correct these errors before anyone sees your document.

Word automatically checks your spelling and grammar as you type. Wavy red underlines indicate possible spelling errors, and wavy blue underlines indicate possible grammar errors. To correct one of these errors on the fly, right-click the underlined text and choose a quick correction from the shortcut menu.

You can also run the full-blown Spelling and Grammar feature within Word to check the entire document at once. One by one, each potential error appears in a dialog box, and you click buttons to decide how to deal with each one.

One of the choices when dealing with a potentially misspelled word is to add the word to the dictionary so that it isn't flagged as misspelled in any future spell check in any document. The Dictionary file is common to all Office applications, so any word you add to the dictionary in Word is no longer flagged as misspelled in Excel, PowerPoint, or Outlook.

Word has a more robust and powerful Spelling and Grammar feature than the other Office applications, but they all have similar functionality. Therefore, after you learn how to check spelling and grammar in Word, you can also do so in the other Office apps.

In the following exercise, you correct spelling and grammar errors in a document.

Files needed: Chapter 2 Spelling.docx

1. **In Word, open the Chapter 2 Spelling file and save it as Chapter 2 Spelling Corrected.**

2. **Right-click the misspelled word *eerors* and on the shortcut menu that appears, choose the correct spelling, *errors* (see Figure 2-21).**

3. **Click at the beginning of the document to move the insertion point there, and then choose Review⇨Spelling & Grammar.**

   The Spelling and Grammar task pane opens, with the first mistake (Grammer) highlighted. See Figure 2-22.

Figure 2-21

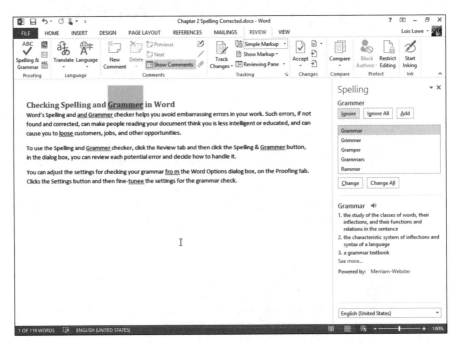

Figure 2-22

4. **Click the Change All button to change all instances of *grammer* to *grammar*.**

   The next mistake found is the duplicate word: *and and.*

5. **Click Delete to delete one of the instances of *and*.**

   The next mistake found is a possible grammar area: the capitalization of *Spelling*. In this case, the capitalization is correct.

6. **Click the Ignore button to skip the correctly capitalized word.**

   The next mistake found is the misuse of *lose* as *loose.*

7. **Click the Change button to change to the correct word.**

   The next mistake found is an extra space in the word *from.*

8. **Click the Change button to remove the extra space.**

   The next mistake is the misspelling of *tune* as *tunee.*

9. **Click the Change button to correct the spelling.**

   A dialog box appears to tell you that the spell check is complete.

10. **Click OK and then save your work.**

Leave the document open for the next exercise.

Sharing Your Document with Others

If the people with whom you want to share your work are also Office users (versions 2007 and higher), sharing with them is easy. Just give them your data file. You can transfer a data file to someone else via a USB drive, a portable disc such as a writable CD or DVD, or e-mail.

To share with people who don't have Office 2007 higher, you can save in other formats. Word (and the other Office apps) supports a variety of saving formats, so you're sure to find a format that bridges the distance between Office and the program that your recipient uses.

E-mailing your document to others

Some versions of Office include *Microsoft Outlook,* an e-mail, calendar, and contact management program. If you don't have Outlook, you might have some other e-mail program. When you send a document via e-mail from within Word, Word calls up your default e-mail application, whatever that may be. The steps in

LINGO

One way to distribute your work to others is to send it to them via e-mail. Your document piggybacks on an e-mail as an attachment. An **attachment** is a file that's separate from the body of the e-mail, travelling along with the e-mail to its destination.

this book assume Outlook 2013 is your default e-mail application; your steps might be different if you use a different e-mail application.

If you use a web-based e-mail application, such as Outlook.com (the web-based version of Outlook), Gmail, or Yahoo! Mail, you can't follow along with the steps in this section. You can still send Word files as e-mail attachments, but you can't initiate the process from within Word. You start a new e-mail message from within the web interface, and then attach the file from there.

In the following exercise, you send a document to yourself as an e-mail attachment. These steps assume that Outlook is your default e-mail program and that your e-mail account is already set up in it.

Files needed: Chapter 2 Spelling Corrected.docx, open from the preceding exercise

1. **In Chapter 2 Spelling Corrected, choose File⇨Share, click Email, and then click Send As Attachment.**

   A new message opens in Outlook (or your default e-mail application) with the Chapter 2 Spelling Corrected file already attached. The filename also appears in the Subject line. See Figure 2-23.

Figure 2-23

2. **Click in the To box and type your own e-mail address there, and then click the Send button.**

   The file is sent to you.

3. **In Outlook, choose Home⇨Send/Receive All Folders.**

   You receive the sent file as a new message in your inbox.

If the message doesn't appear right away, click Send/Receive All Folders again.

4. **Close Outlook and return to Word.**

5. **Close the document (but not Word), saving your changes if prompted.**

Leave Word open for the next exercise.

Sharing your document in other formats

If your intended recipients use earlier versions of Office or don't have Office at all, you must save your work in another format before transferring the file to them. All the Office programs allow you to export your work in other formats, so you can transfer just about any data to just about any other application.

The further away you get from the original version of the file, the more formatting features you lose. For example, saving in the Word 2010 format preserves the most features, and saving in Word 97–2003 format loses some features. RTF loses even more, and plain text loses all formatting.

In the following exercise, you save a file in two formats.

Files needed: Chapter 2 Distribution.docx

1. **In Word, open the Chapter 2 Distribution file and choose File⇨Save As.**

   The Save As page of Backstage view opens.

2. **Click the location where you want to save the file (your SkyDrive or Computer) and then click Browse to open the Save As dialog box.**

3. **From the Save As Type drop-down list, choose Word 97–2003 Document (see Figure 2-24) and then click Save.**

   Your document is saved in a format that's compatible with earlier Word versions (Word 97 through Word 2003); it's also usable in Word 2007 and Word 2010.

Figure 2-24

4. **Choose File⇨Save As, and click Browse to reopen the Save As dialog box.**

5. **Open the Save as Type drop-down list and choose Rich Text Format.**

6. **Click the Save button.**

Your document is saved in Rich Text Format. This format is useful for exchanging data with someone who has a different brand of word processor, such as WordPerfect.

Leave the document open for the next exercise.

Printing Your Work

Another way to distribute your work is by printing it, provided you have access to a printer. You can do a quick print with the default settings, or you can specify a certain printer, number of copies, page range, and other settings.

In the following exercise, you print a document.

Files needed: Chapter 2 Distribution.docx, open from the preceding exercise

1. **In Chapter 2 Distribution, choose File⇨Print.**

   The Print page of Backstage view appears.

2. **In the Copies box, click the up arrow once to change the number to 2. Then click the down arrow to change it back to 1.**

3. **Open the Printer drop-down list and choose the printer you want to use (see Figure 2-25).**

> For more practice, check out the additional print options. For example, you can change the page range, orientation, paper size, margins, and duplex setting (that is, print one-sided or two-sided). The settings for duplex and collation, as well as for printing only specific pages, don't apply to the document used in this exercise because it has only one page.

4. **Click the Print button.**

   The document prints.

Exit Word.

Figure 2-25

Want more help learning the basics of Word document creation and editing? You can find Word tutorials here: `http://office.microsoft.com/en-us/word-help/CH010369478.aspx`.

Summing Up

Word makes it easy to create a basic document. You can either start typing in the blank document that opens automatically at startup, or choose one of the templates provided. Here are the key points this chapter covered:

- To start a new blank document, press Ctrl+N, or choose File⇨New and then click Blank Document.

- To start a document based on a template, choose File⇨New, pick the template you want, and then click Create.

- To set page margins, choose Page Layout⇨Margins.

- To change the paper size, choose Page Layout⇨Size.

- Portrait and Landscape are the two page orientations. Portrait is the default. To switch, choose Page Layout⇨Orientation⇨Landscape.

- To find text, use the Navigation pane; press Ctrl+F to open it, or choose Home⇨Find.

- To replace text, use the Find and Replace dialog box; Ctrl+H opens it, or choose Home⇨Replace.

- To sort a list, select the list and choose Home⇨Sort.

- Word checks spelling and grammar automatically, and underlines errors with a red wavy underline (for spelling) or a blue wavy underline (for grammar).

- You can also launch a full spelling and grammar check by choosing Review⇨Spelling & Grammar.

- To e-mail your document to others, choose File⇨Save & Send and then click Send As Attachment.

- To print your document, choose File⇨Print.

Try-it-yourself lab

For more practice with the features covered in this chapter, try the following exercise on your own:

1. **Start Word and write a description of a funny or embarrassing incident that happened recently to you or someone you know.**

2. **Add a new paragraph at the beginning of the document and type a title there, such as** My Most Embarrassing Day Ever**.**

3. **Check your spelling and grammar, and then make any corrections needed.**

4. **E-mail the document to yourself or to a friend you want to share it with.**

5. **Print one copy of the document and then close Word.**

Know this tech talk

ascending: A to Z order. Numbers and symbols precede letters.

attachment: A file attached to an e-mail so that the file is sent along with the message.

descending: Z to A order. Numbers and symbols follow letters.

landscape: A page orientation in which the wide part of the paper forms the top and bottom.

margins: The space between the edge of the paper and the text.

orientation: The direction the text runs on a piece of paper where one dimension is greater than the other. See also *portrait* and *landscape.*

portrait: A page orientation in which the narrow part of the paper forms the top and bottom.

Chapter 3
Formatting Text

✔ Formatting text *makes your documents more attractive and readable.* You can apply different fonts, sizes, and colors, as well as use style sets and themes to automate the process of formatting an entire document.

✔ Themes *make it easier to apply consistent formatting* within a document and between documents.

✔ WordArt enables you to easily *format text with fancy special effects* that blur the line between text formatting and artwork.

✔ Custom character spacing and scale settings *provide precise control for professional-quality typesetting.*

*W*ithout formatting, text can be dull and dreary. You'll probably want to pep up your prose by applying various fonts, attributes, colors, and themes to capture your readers' interest.

In this chapter, I explain how to format text in a Word document. By the end of this chapter, you'll be able to choose fonts, sizes, and colors that are appropriate for the job at hand. You'll know how to copy and clear formatting from text. You also find out how to use WordArt to make text extra-special, and how to adjust typographical settings that can make text look like it was professionally typeset.

Formatting Text

Text formatting can make a big difference in the readability of a document. By making certain text larger, boldface, or a different font, you can call attention to it and add interest for your readers.

You can apply each type of character formatting individually, or you can use style sets or themes to apply multiple types of formatting at once.

<blockquote>
LINGO

The type of formatting covered in this chapter is commonly known as character formatting (formatting that can be applied to individual characters). Character formatting includes fonts, font sizes, text attributes (such as italic), character spacing (spacing between letters), and text color.
</blockquote>

Choosing text font, size, and color

The text in the document appears using a certain style of lettering, dubbed a *font* or *typeface*. Word comes with dozens of fonts, so you're sure to find one that meets the needs of whatever project you create.

Each font is available in a wide variety of sizes measured in *points*, with each point being $\frac{1}{72}$ of an inch on a printout. (The size it appears onscreen depends on the display zoom. You

<blockquote>
LINGO

The style of lettering is a font, or typeface. Fonts are measured in points. Fonts can be in standard colors, which don't change when you change a document theme, or in theme colors, which change with the theme.
</blockquote>

learn about zoom in Chapter 1.) Text sizes vary from very small (6 points) to very large (100 points or more). An average document uses body text that's between 10 and 12 points, and headings between 12 and 18 points.

You can also color each font by using either a *standard color,* which doesn't change when you change document themes, or a *theme color,* which does change. Later in the chapter, you learn how to change themes and you see what happens to the text colors you've applied when the theme colors change.

You can apply fonts, sizes, and colors either from the Home tab of the Ribbon or from the Mini Toolbar.

In the following exercise, you format some text by applying different fonts, sizes, and colors to it.

Files needed: Chapter 3 Vacation.docx

1. **In Word, open Chapter 3 Vacation and save it as Chapter 3 Vacation Formatting.**

2. **Place the insertion point at the beginning of the document, press Enter to create a new paragraph, press the up-arrow key once to move the insertion point into the new paragraph, and then type** Our Vacation.

3. **Triple-click Our Vacation to select the entire paragraph.**

4. **Point the mouse pointer at the selected paragraph so that the Mini Toolbar appears, as shown in Figure 3-1.**

5. **From the Font drop-down list on the Mini Toolbar, choose Arial Black; from the Font Size drop-down list, choose 14.**

Figure 3-1

If the Mini Toolbar is no longer visible, right-click the text to make the Mini Toolbar reappear.

For more practice, change the font and font size by using the controls on the Home tab in the Font group on the Ribbon.

6. **On the Ribbon, choose Home⇨Increase Font Size to increase the font size of the selected text to 16 points (see Figure 3-2).**

Increase Font Size button

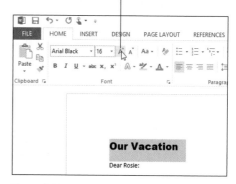

7. **Click the Font Color button.**

Whatever color was already displayed on the button is applied to the text. (The color that appears depends on the most recently used font color.)

8. **Click the down arrow to the right of the Font Color button, and in the palette of colors that appears (see Figure 3-3), click the red square under Standard Colors.**

The text becomes red.

9. **Click the down arrow on the Font Color button again to reopen the color palette, and then click the Orange, Accent 6 square on the top row of the Theme Colors section.**

Figure 3-2

Font Color button

Red square

Figure 3-3

Pointing at a square makes its name appear in a ScreenTip.

For more practice, try some of the tints and shades below the theme colors.

LINGO

A **tint** is a lighter version of a color, and a **shade** is a darker version of it.

Leave the document open for the next exercise.

Applying text attributes and WordArt effects

You can modify text with a variety of *attributes,* such as bold, italic, underlining, and so on. You can apply some of these from the Mini Toolbar and/or the Font group on the Home tab. Others are available in the Font dialog box. Some of them also have keyboard shortcuts.

Table 3-1 summarizes the keyboard shortcuts for some common text formatting attributes. Figure 3-4 displays some of these attributes.

LINGO

Attributes are typographical styles such as bold, italic, and underline. **Text effects,** or **WordArt effects,** are special types of effects, such as reflection or glow, that are unique to Office applications.

Table 3-1	Keyboard Shortcuts for Applying Text Attributes
Attribute	*Keyboard Shortcut*
Bold	Ctrl+B
Italic	Ctrl+I
Underline	Ctrl+U
Subscript	Ctrl+=
Superscript	Ctrl+Shift++ (plus sign)
Underline words but not spaces	Ctrl+Shift+W
Double underline text	Ctrl+Shift+D
Small caps	Ctrl+Shift+K
All caps	Ctrl+Shift+A

Bold	*Italics*	<u>Underline</u>
Super^script^	Sub~script~	~~Strikethrough~~
Small Caps	ALL CAPS	~~Double Strikethrough~~

Figure 3-4

You can apply *text effects,* or *WordArt effects,* such as outline, shadow, reflection, and glow. Figure 3-5 shows some examples of these effects, accessed from the Text Effects button's menu on the Home tab. The Text Effects button's menu also includes a number of presets that combine color fills, outlines, and other effects in one operation.

Outline   Shadow

Glow   Reflection

Figure 3-5

In the following exercise, you format some text by applying some attributes and effects to it.

Files needed: Chapter 3 Vacation Formatting.docx, open from the preceding exercise

1. **In Chapter 3 Vacation Formatting, triple-click the Our Vacation title to select it if it's not already selected.**

2. **Choose Home⇨Text Effects and Typography (see Figure 3-6), and then click the second sample in the bottom row.**

   The text becomes black with a blue shadow.

3. **Click the Text Effects button again, point to Glow, and click the first effect in the Glow Variations section (see Figure 3-7).**

Choose this sample.

Figure 3-6

Click this variation.

Figure 3-7

4. **Choose Home⇨Italic to italicize the text, and then click the dialog box launcher in the lower-right corner of the Font group on the Home tab (see Figure 3-8).**

   The Font dialog box opens.

Dialog box launcher

Figure 3-8

5. **Select the Small Caps check box, as shown in Figure 3-9, and then click OK.**

6. **Save your work.**

Leave the document open for the next exercise.

Figure 3-9

Working with Themes

Themes enable you to dramatically change the look of a document quickly. They apply several types of preset formatting to text, including font, color, and object formatting. In a Word document that contains only text, you won't notice the effect changes when you switch to a different theme, but the font and color changes will be apparent.

TIP All the Office applications use the same set of themes, so themes can help you standardize the look of your work across multiple applications. For example, you could make the fonts and colors on a brochure you create in Word similar to a presentation you create in PowerPoint.

LINGO

A **theme** is a file that contains settings for fonts (heading and body), colors, and object formatting effects (such as 3-D effects for drawn shapes and SmartArt diagrams, both of which you learn about in later chapters). Themes enable you to dramatically change the look of a document quickly.

You can also apply color themes, font themes, and/or effect themes separately. This ability is useful when none of the available themes exactly match what you want. After you select the right combination of colors, fonts, and effects, you can save your choices as a new theme to use in other documents (including in Excel, PowerPoint, and Word).

REMEMBER

Themes affect only text that hasn't had manual formatting applied that overrides the defaults. For example, if you've specified a certain font or font color for some text, that text doesn't change when you change the theme. You can strip off manual formatting with the Clear All Formatting button on the Home tab.

In the following exercise, you change the document's formatting by applying a different theme, theme fonts, and theme colors.

Files needed: Chapter 3 Vacation Formatting.docx, open from the preceding exercise

1. In the Chapter 3 Vacation Formatting file, choose Design⇨Themes, and in the list of themes that appears (see Figure 3-10), choose Damask.

The colors and fonts in the document change to match the theme.

> **EXTRA INFO**
>
> To use a theme that someone else has given you, choose Design⇨Themes⇨Browse for Themes. You can then specify the location where the theme file is stored.

Damask

Figure 3-10

Point the mouse at several other themes and see their effects in the text behind the open menu.

2. **Click the Fonts button, and in the list of available theme font sets that appears (see Figure 3-11), choose Calibri Light-Constantia.**

   The fonts in the document change.

Point the mouse at several other font themes and see their effects in the text behind the open menu.

Figure 3-11

3. **Click the Colors button, and in the list of available theme color sets that appears (see Figure 3-12), choose Green Yellow.**

   The color of the glow around the heading changes to green.

4. **Save your work.**

Leave the document open for the next exercise.

Figure 3-12

Applying Style Sets

At the top of the Font drop-down list on the Home tab are two entries: one designated for headings and one for body text. If you use these settings rather than specifying individual fonts, you can reformat the document by choosing a different style set.

TIP If you've manually applied specific fonts, you won't see a change when you apply a different style set. If you don't get the results you expect with a style set, select the entire document (press Ctrl+A), and then clear the formatting by clicking the Clear Formatting button on the Home tab or by pressing Ctrl+space bar.

LINGO

A **style set** is a preset combination of fonts, paragraph line spacing, character spacing, and indentation. Style sets enable you to quickly change the look of the document without manually reformatting each paragraph.

In the following exercise, you change the style set.

Files needed: Chapter 3 Vacation Formatting.docx, open from the preceding exercise

1. **In the Chapter 3 Vacation Formatting file, triple-click the Our Vacation title to select it, if it's not already selected.**

2. **Choose Home⇨Clear All Formatting to remove all the formatting you've applied to the selected text.**

   See Figure 3-13. Notice that the manual formatting is cleared, but the font choice from the theme applied in the preceding exercise remains.

3. **From the Font drop-down list, click Calibri Light (Headings) at the top of the list.**

   The Our Vacation text changes to the Calibri Light font.

Clear All Formatting button

Figure 3-13

TIP

If you did not complete the preceding exercise, some other font may appear at the top of the list, with (Headings) next to it. If so, choose that font. The important part is that you choose the font with (Headings) next to it.

4. **Select the rest of the document (everything except the Our Vacation paragraph). Then open the Font drop-down list and select Constantia (Body) at the top of the list.**

5. **Click the Design tab on the Ribbon and then click the More button in the Document Formatting group. (It's the down-arrow button with the horizontal line over the arrow.)**

   A list of available style sets appears. See Figure 3-14.

Pointing to an item allows you to preview it. Point to each of the style sets on the Style Set menu, one by one, and watch the document's formatting change.

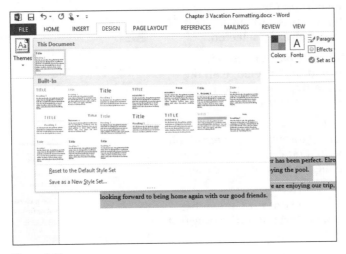

Figure 3-14

6. Choose Lines (Distinctive).

The Lines (Distinctive) style set is applied.

7. Triple-click the Our Vacation heading and change the font size to 18 points. Then click away from the text to deselect it.

The document looks like Figure 3-15.

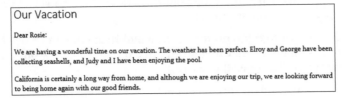

Our Vacation

Dear Rosie:

We are having a wonderful time on our vacation. The weather has been perfect. Elroy and George have been collecting seashells, and Judy and I have been enjoying the pool.

California is certainly a long way from home, and although we are enjoying our trip, we are looking forward to being home again with our good friends.

Figure 3-15

8. Save your work and close the document.

Leave Word open for the next exercise.

Copying Formats with Format Painter

When many blocks of text need to be formatted the same way, it can be tedious to select and format each block. As a shortcut, Word offers the Format Painter feature. Format Painter picks up the formatting from one block of text and applies it to another.

If you select the destination text, Format Painter copies only *character-based formatting* (that is, the type of formatting created by the commands in the Font group of the Home tab). If you click in a paragraph as the destination, rather than selecting specific text, Word copies both character and paragraph settings. Paragraph settings include things like left and right indents, tab stops, and spacing between lines.

In the following exercise, you copy the formatting from one block of text to another.

Files needed: Chapter 3 Jobs.docx

Format Painter button

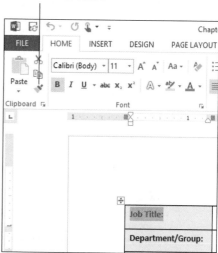

1. **Open Chapter 3 Jobs and save it as Chapter 3 Jobs Formatting.**

2. **Click and drag the mouse pointer across the text *Job Title* to select it, and then choose Home⇨Format Painter (see Figure 3-16).**

3. **Click and drag across the text *Department/Group:* to paint the formatting onto that text.**

   The Format Painter feature turns itself off automatically.

4. **With the *Department/Group:* text still selected, double-click the Format Painter button.**

   Figure 3-16

   Double-clicking Format Painter rather than just clicking it once turns it on so that it remains on until you turn it off.

5. **Drag across each of the other headings in the blue-background boxes, one after the other.**

   The formatting is copied to each of those blocks of text. When you're finished, the formatting looks like Figure 3-17.

Job Posting			
Anderson Supplies, Incorporated			
Job Title:	Controller	Job Category:	Financial
Department/Group:	Accounting	Job Code:	58374
Level/Salary Range:	$75,000 to $90,000	Position Type:	Full-time
Job Description			

Figure 3-17

6. **Click the Format Painter button to turn off the feature, and then save your work.**

Leave the document open for the next exercise.

Customizing Characters and Their Spacing

Word processing has certainly come a long way since the days of the type-writer. In some cases, you may want to adjust Word's automatic character spacing to create special effects.

Nowadays you can also fine-tune the characters in your document as pre-cisely as the most high-end typesetting equipment of 20 years ago. Even though Word isn't considered a high-end desktop publishing program like QuarkXPress or Adobe InDesign, it still has several features for adjusting the typesetting in your document.

Adjusting character spacing

Text scale and spacing changes can help you fit your text into an available space by subtly changing the spacing between each letter. It may not be obvious to your reader that you've made such a change, but the overall effect is to increase or decrease the amount of space that text occupies on the page.

LINGO

Character spacing refers to the spacing between individual char-acters, and also secondarily to a character's individual vertical positioning, such as with super-script and subscript.

The Scale setting controls the width of each character. Changing the scale makes the characters wider or narrower in relation to their height. For example, Figure 3-18 shows the same text at 80-, 100-, and 150-percent scaling. The 150-percent version looks like it's taller than the others, but that's an optical illusion; they're actually all the same height — only the width changes.

On Sale Now 80%

On Sale Now 100%

On Sale Now 150%

Figure 3-18

The Spacing setting controls the blank space between letters. For example, Figure 3-19 shows the same text with different amounts of spacing. Condensed spacing jams the letters together; expanded spacing spreads them out. These examples are dramatic to show the differences more clearly, but in most documents, an adjustment of one point or less may be sufficient.

Condensed by 1.7 points

Normal Spacing

Expanded by 1.7 points

Figure 3-19

In this exercise, you adjust the text scale and text spacing.

Files needed: Chapter 3 Jobs Formatting.docx, open from the preceding exercise

1. **In Chapter 3 Jobs Formatting, scroll down to the bottom of the document.**

   Notice that the text doesn't quite fit on one page.

2. **Select all the text in the bottom table cell, beginning with the Job Purpose heading.**

3. **On the Home tab, click the dialog box launcher in the Font group (see Figure 3-20).**

   The Font dialog box opens.

Dialog box launcher

Figure 3-20

4. **In the Font dialog box, click the Advanced tab; from the Scale drop-down list, choose 90% (see Figure 3-21), and then click OK.**

Figure 3-21

5. **Scroll to the bottom of the page to see whether the text all fits on one page now, and then click the dialog box launcher for the Font group to reopen the Font dialog box.**

6. **From the Scale drop-down list, choose 100% to restore the text's original spacing; from the Spacing drop-down list, choose Condensed; in the By box next to Spacing, click the up arrow to set the amount of condensing to 0.4 point (see Figure 3-22), and then click OK.**

 You'd think that clicking the up arrow would increase the amount of the setting, but because it's condensing the text, a smaller number makes it *less* condensed. So the number goes down as you click the up arrow.

7. **Scroll again to the bottom of the document and notice that the text fits on one page.**

8. **Save the document.**

Leave the document open for the next exercise.

Set the amount by which
to condense the spacing.

Figure 3-22

Enabling kerning

Kerning decreases the space between certain pairs of letters based on their shapes. Kerning can make a visual difference when two large letters are adjacent to each other and their shapes happen to fit together, such as a V and an A. Kerning places them closer together than they typically would be, so it doesn't look like there is too much space between them. Kerning is typically done only when the text is over a certain point size because at smaller sizes, it's not noticeable. Figure 3-23 shows examples of kerned and unkerned text in Times New Roman at 100 points in size.

> **LINGO**
>
> **Kerning** is a spacing adjustment made between two letters based on their shapes.

In this exercise, you enable kerning for text 18 points and larger.

Files needed: Chapter 3 Jobs Formatting.docx, open from the preceding exercise

1. **In Chapter 3 Jobs Formatting, triple-click the Job Posting heading at the top of the page to select it.**

2. **On the Home tab, click the dialog box launcher in the Font group.**

   The Font dialog box opens.

3. **On the Advanced tab, click the Kerning for Fonts *xx* Points and Above check box but leave the default setting of 18 points as-is (see Figure 3-24). Click OK.**

   The selected text is kerned. The difference is subtle, so you might not notice the change.

4. **Save the document.**

Leave the document open for the next exercise.

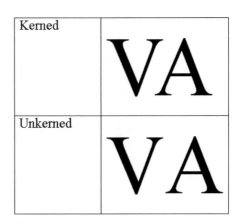

Figure 3-23

Enable kerning.

Figure 3-24

Creating custom superscript and subscript

You can change the vertical position of a character, moving it up or down in relation to the other characters around it. This is useful, for example, when you want to adjust the position of a superscript or subscript character. By adjusting the character position, you can increase or decrease the amount of raising or lowering.

LINGO

Superscript characters are raised a certain amount above the baseline, and **subscript** characters are lowered a certain amount.

In this exercise, you adjust the position of a superscript numeral.

Files needed: Chapter 3 Jobs Formatting.docx, open from the preceding exercise

1. **In Chapter 3 Jobs Formatting, click to move the insertion point after $90,000 on the third row of the table, and then type** 1.

2. **Select the 1 you just typed, and choose Home⇨Superscript to make the character smaller and raise it above the baseline (see Figure 3-25).**

   Note the position of the 1 in relation to the adjacent 0.

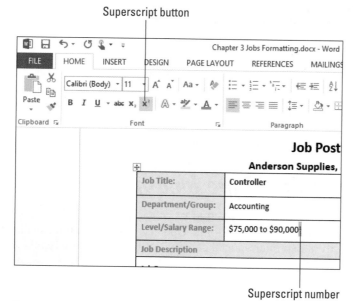

Figure 3-25

3. **With the 1 still selected, click the dialog box launcher for the Font group, opening the Font dialog box.**

4. On the Advanced tab, from the Position drop-down list, choose Raised. In the By box, leave the default setting of 3 points as-is (see Figure 3-26), and click OK.

Figure 3-26

Notice that the 1 is now significantly higher than the 0 adjacent to it. See Figure 3-27.

5. Save the document.

Leave the document open for the next exercise.

$75,000 to $90,000[1]

Figure 3-27

Controlling OpenType font options

OpenType is a kind of font file that Windows and Macintosh computers use. Like the older TrueType fonts, OpenType fonts are fully scalable to any size, but they also offer special capabilities for fine-tuning typeface settings, such as

✓ **Ligatures:** A *ligature* is a combination of characters that's written as a *glyph,* that is, as though the characters together are a single character. Most often ligatures are made up of pairs of letters, such as when the lowercase letter *f* is combined with others. Look at the two lowercase *fs* in the word *different* in Figure 3-28; the first instance of *different* does not use a ligature, and the second one does. In the ligature version, the horizontal lines on the *fs* are fused.

✔ **Number spacing:** Number character spacing can be either *proportional* (in which numbers are spaced like letters, with varying widths) or *tabular* (in which each number has the same width). Each font has a default setting, but you can override it.

✔ **Number forms:** Numbers can be either *lining* (not extending below the baseline of the text, and all the same height) or *oldstyle* (extending below the baseline or centered higher on the line). Each font has a default setting, but you can override it.

✔ **Stylistic sets:** Some fonts contain multiple *stylistic sets* (up to 20), which contain alternatively formed versions of some characters. You can choose among the stylistic sets that a font provides (if any). This is different from Word's style sets. See Figure 3-29.

✔ **Contextual Alternates:** This feature, when enabled, changes the shapes of letters or combinations of letters based on surrounding characters. This can be used to make script fonts look more natural and flowing, or to use alternative letter forms at the start or end of words or next to punctuation.

Different

Different

Figure 3-28

Stylistic Set 1

Stylistic Set 2

Stylistic Set 3

Stylistic Set 4

Figure 3-29

GO ONLINE

For more information about OpenType features in Word, see `http://office.microsoft.com/en-us/word-help/opentype-options-in-the-font-dialog-box-HA101809106.aspx`.

Not all OpenType fonts include all these features. The Calibri, Cambria, Candara, Consolas, Constantia, and Corbel fonts all contain various OpenType features, as does Gabriola, a font that comes with Windows 7. If you have Gabriola available, it's the best one to experiment with because it contains the most OpenType features.

In this exercise, you modify OpenType options.

Files needed: Chapter 3 Jobs Formatting.docx, open from the preceding exercise

1. In Chapter 3 Jobs Formatting, select the two paragraphs of text above the table.

2. On the Home tab, click the dialog box launcher to open the Font dialog box.

3. In the Font dialog box that appears, on the Advanced tab, open the Ligatures drop-down list, choose All, and click OK.

   Notice that now the *t* and the *i* in *Posting* run together.

4. Press Ctrl+Z to undo the action to see how it looked before applying the ligature; then press Ctrl+Y to redo the action to reapply the ligature.

5. Select the salary range ($75,000 to $90,000[1]), and then click the dialog box launcher in the Font group to reopen the Font dialog box.

6. In the Font dialog box, on the Advanced tab, from the Number Spacing drop-down list, choose Proportional, review the sample in the bottom of the dialog box to see how the text will change, and then click OK to apply the change.

7. Select the job code (58374), and then click the dialog box launcher in the Font group to reopen the Font dialog box.

8. In the Font dialog box, on the Advanced tab, from the Number Forms drop-down list, choose Old-Style, review the sample in the bottom of the dialog box to see how the text will change, and click OK.

9. Save the document and close it.

Exit Word.

Summing Up

Word makes it easy to create a basic document. You can either start typing in the blank document that opens automatically at startup or choose one of the templates provided. Here are the key points this chapter covered:

- ✔ Fonts, or typefaces, are lettering styles. Choose a font from the Home tab or from the Mini Toolbar.

- ✔ Font sizes are measured in points. A point is ½₂ of an inch. Choose font sizes from the Home tab or from the Mini Toolbar.

- ✔ A style set applies a different appearance to a document, including fonts, paragraph spacing, character spacing, and indentation. To change the style set, choose Home⇨Change Styles⇨Style Set.

- ✔ Some text attributes and effects can be applied from the Mini Toolbar or the Font group on the Home tab. Others must be applied from the Font dialog box. To open the Font dialog box, click the dialog box launcher in the Font group.

✔ A theme is a file that contains settings for fonts, colors, and object formatting effects. Apply a theme by choosing Design➪Themes.

✔ Scale is the width of each character; spacing is the blank space between characters.

✔ You can control scale and spacing on the Advanced tab of the Font dialog box. Click the dialog box launcher for the Font group to access it.

✔ Kerning adjusts spacing between two characters based on their shapes.

✔ Some OpenType fonts offer special typesetting options. For example, a ligature is a combination of characters that's written as though the characters are a single character.

Try-it-yourself lab

For more practice with the features covered in this chapter, try the following exercise on your own:

1. **Open the file Chapter 3 Summary.docx and save the file as Chapter 3 Try It.docx.**
2. **Change the style set to Shaded, and then change the theme to Ion.**
3. **Select the entire document and clear all manual formatting from it.**
4. **Apply the Cambria font to the body text of the article, and then condense the body text by 0.5 point.**
5. **Enable ligatures of all types, and then set the scale on the title (Wuthering Heights) to 150 percent.**
6. **Close Word, saving all changes when prompted.**

Know this tech talk

attributes: Formatting options such as bold, italic, and underline.

character formatting: Formatting that affects only individual characters, such as font choices. Contrast this to paragraph formatting, such as indentation and line spacing, that affects entire paragraphs.

character spacing: The spacing between the individual characters in a paragraph.

effects: Special WordArt-style effects, such as glow, reflection, and shadow, applied to text.

font: Also called a *typeface*. A style of lettering, such as Arial, Times New Roman, or Calibri.

ligature: The combination of two letters together, forming a glyph (or graphic).

lining number form: Numbers that begin at the baseline and are of the same height.

old-style number form: Numbers that may be above or below the baseline and may be different heights.

OpenType: An advanced type of scalable font that includes special typesetting features.

point: A unit of measure that's $\frac{1}{2}$ of an inch. Font size is measured in points.

proportional spacing: Spacing that's dependent on the width of the character.

scale: The setting that modifies the width of each character from its default of 100 percent.

spacing: A setting that controls the blank space between letters.

standard color: A fixed color that doesn't change when you change to a different theme.

style set: A set of font, indentation, and line spacing options.

stylistic set: An alternative set of characters stored in an OpenType font file, dictating different looks for certain characters.

tabular spacing: Spacing that's the same for every character.

template: An example file on which new documents may be based.

theme: A set of font, color, and graphic effect settings stored in a separate file, accessible to all Office applications.

theme color: A set of color choices that are applied to color placeholders in a document.

typeface: See *font*.

Chapter 4
Formatting Paragraphs

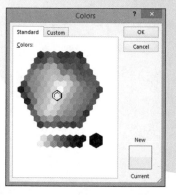

- Paragraph formatting enables you to *control the indentation, line spacing, and horizontal alignment* of a paragraph.

- *Indenting a paragraph can set it off visually* from the rest of the document for greater emphasis.

- *To make a text-heavy document easier to read,* increase its line spacing so that more space appears between each line.

- Custom tab stops enable you to *control the position the insertion point moves into* when you press the Tab key.

- Create a numbered list to *organize a list in which the order of the items is significant;* use a bulleted list when the order is not significant.

- Adding a border or shading to a paragraph makes it *stand out from the rest of the document.*

*P*aragraphs are essential building blocks in a Word document. Each time you press Enter, you start a new paragraph. If you've ever seen a document where the author didn't use paragraph breaks, you know how important paragraphs can be. Breaking the content into logical chunks helps the reader understand your meaning.

Formatting your paragraphs helps anyone reading your documents even more, and you explore how in this chapter. First, make sure you understand a few basics:

✔ Paragraph formatting is formatting that affects whole paragraphs and cannot be applied to individual characters. For example, line spacing is a type of paragraph formatting, along with indentation and alignment.

✔ How paragraph formatting is applied depends on what you've selected:

- *If you apply paragraph formatting when no text is selected,* the formatting applies to the paragraph in which the insertion point is currently located.

- *If you apply paragraph formatting when text is selected,* the formatting applies to whatever paragraphs are included in that selection, even if only one character of the paragraph is included.

It's quick and easy to select multiple paragraphs at once and then format them as a group.

To set the paragraph formatting for the entire document at once, press Ctrl+A to select the entire document and then issue the paragraph formatting commands.

In this chapter, you learn how to apply various types of formatting to paragraphs. For example, you learn how to adjust the spacing and alignment of a paragraph, how to create bulleted and numbered lists, and how to manage tab stops and indents. You also find out how to spotlight a paragraph by adding a border and shading to it.

Aligning Paragraphs

Most of the time, aligning paragraphs refers to *horizontal alignment,* or where the paragraph aligns in relation to the right and left margins. In Word, your choices are Align Text Left, Align Text Right, Center, and Justify. Figure 4-1 shows an example of each of the alignment types.

Figure 4-1

Each of those is pretty self-evident except the last one. *Justify* aligns both the left and right sides of the paragraph with the margins, stretching out or compressing the text in each line as needed to make it fit. The final line in the paragraph is exempt and appears left-aligned.

If you apply Justify alignment to a paragraph that contains only one line, it looks like it's left-aligned. However, if you then type more text into the paragraph so it wraps to additional lines, the Justify alignment becomes apparent.

LINGO

Horizontal alignment refers to the positioning of the paragraph between the right and left margins. **Vertical alignment** refers to how paragraphs are positioned between the top and bottom margins. Most documents start at the top, but you can align documents to the center or bottom of your document, too. You might use this feature if you're creating a cover page, for example, or a business letter. Chapter 6, which is all about formatting special pages and sections, covers vertical alignment.

In the following exercise, you apply horizontal alignment changes to a business letter.

Files needed: Chapter 4 Time Out.docx

1. **In Word, open Chapter 4 Time Out from the data files for this chapter and save it as Chapter 4 Time Out Letter.**

2. **Select the first three lines (the facility's name and address) and then choose Home⇨Center or press Ctrl+E (see Figure 4-2).**

Center button

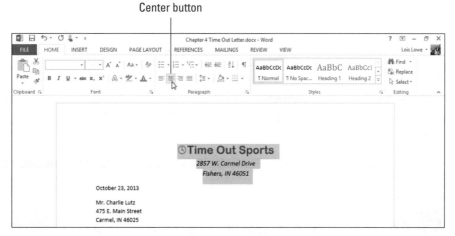

Figure 4-2

3. **Click in the first body paragraph (the paragraph that starts with *"Thank you . . ."*) and then choose Home⇨Justify or press Ctrl+J.**

   The paragraph changes to Justify alignment.

4. **Select the last four body paragraphs of the document (starting with *"Our sales and support staff . . ."*) and click the Justify button again.**

   Those paragraphs change to Justify alignment. Figure 4-3 shows the results.

5. **Save the changes to the document.**

Leave the document open for the next exercise.

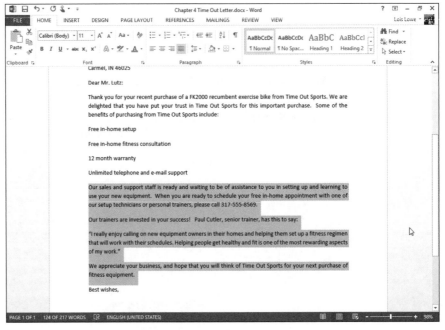

Figure 4-3

Spacing Lines and Paragraphs

A paragraph has three values you can set for its spacing:

- ✔ **Line spacing** is the space between the lines within a multiline paragraph.
- ✔ **Before** is extra spacing added above the first line of the paragraph.
- ✔ **After** is extra spacing added below the last line of the paragraph.

You can set line spacing to any of several presets such as Single, Double, and 1.5 Lines, or to an exact value measured in points. You may remember from Chapter 3 that a *point* is 1/72 of an inch. Space before and after a paragraph is specified in points, too.

LINGO

Vertical spacing refers to the amount of space (also known as the **leading**) between each line. The first part of the word *leading* is pronounced like the hazardous metal common in old houses (not like the abbreviation for *leader* on a business project).

If you specify an exact amount of space per line and you change the font size, the text may not look right anymore. For example, if you change the font size to a larger size than the exact spacing is set for, the lines might overlap vertically. If you aren't sure what font sizes you need, don't use exact spacing.

In the following exercise, you change the vertical spacing for paragraphs in a letter.

Files needed: Chapter 4 Time Out Letter.docx, open from the preceding exercise

1. **In the Chapter 4 Time Out Letter document, press Ctrl+A to select the entire document.**

2. **Choose Home⇨Line Spacing⇨1.0 (see Figure 4-4).**

   The line spacing in every paragraph changes to single spacing.

   Line Spacing button

Figure 4-4

3. **Select the paragraph beginning with *"Free in-home setup . . ."* and the next two paragraphs following it.**

4. **Click the Line Spacing button again and then choose Remove Space After Paragraph (see Figure 4-5).**

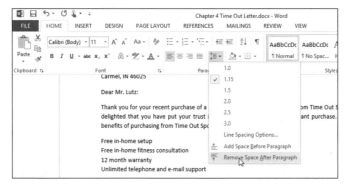

Figure 4-5

5. **Select the Time Out Sports heading at the top of the document.**

6. **Click the Line Spacing button again and choose Line Spacing Options.**

   The Paragraph dialog box opens.

> **TIP**
> You can also click the dialog box launcher for the Paragraph group to open the Paragraph dialog box if you prefer that method.

7. **Decrease the value in the After text box to 6 pt (see Figure 4-6) and then click OK to accept the new setting.**

Set the After value to 6 pt.

Figure 4-6

8. **Triple-click the quotation paragraph to select it, and then click the Line Spacing button again and choose Line Spacing Options.**

   The Paragraph dialog box opens again.

9. **From the Line Spacing drop-down list, choose Exactly; then type 15 into the text box to its right (see Figure 4-7) and click OK.**

Set Line Spacing to exactly 15 pt.

Figure 4-7

For more practice, set the font size for the paragraph you just formatted to 24 points and watch what happens to the line spacing; it stays at 15 points, and the lines overlap. Press Ctrl+Z to undo when you're finished experimenting.

10. **Save the changes to the document.**

Leave the document open for the next exercise.

Indenting a Paragraph

When you want to emphasize a paragraph, such as a quote, by setting it off from the body text, turn to Word's indent features.

If you're new to indentation, here's what you need to know:

- ✔ **When a paragraph has no indentation,** it's allowed to take up the full range of space between the left and right margins.

- ✔ **When you set indentation for a paragraph,** its left and/or right sides are inset by the amount you specify, as shown in Figure 4-8.

> Here is a quotation about travel by Francis Bacon, a writer and philosopher who lived from 1561 to 1626:
>
> > Travel, in the younger sort, is a part of education; in the elder, a part of experience. He that travelleth into a country before he hath some entrance into the language, goeth to school, and not to travel.

Figure 4-8

In addition to a left and right indent value, each paragraph can optionally have a special indent for the first line:

- ✔ **A first-line indent (clever name) occurs when the first line is indented more than the rest of the paragraph.** You're probably familiar with first-line indents from reading novels or reports. To help the reader's eye catch the beginning of a paragraph, most long documents use either a first-line indent or extra vertical space between paragraphs (not both).

- ✔ **A hanging indent occurs when the first line is indented less than the rest of the paragraph.** Hanging indents are typically used to create listings. In a bulleted or numbered list, the bullet or number hangs off the left edge of the paragraph in a hanging indent. However, in Word, when you create bulleted or numbered lists (covered later in this chapter), Word adjusts the paragraph's hanging indent automatically, so you don't have to think about it.

LINGO

Indentation is the amount that a paragraph is inset in relation to the left and right margins. A **first-line indent** is present when the first line's indentation is more than that of the subsequent lines. A **hanging indent** is the reverse — the first line is indented less than the other lines.

Applying indents

Word has two main tools for indenting paragraphs:

✔ **The Decrease Indent and Increase Indent buttons on the Home tab:** The Home tab offers a quick and easy way to indent a paragraph along the left margin.

✔ **The Paragraph dialog box:** Here, you can apply first-line or hanging indents and set precise amounts of indentation for the left or right margins.

In the following exercise, you apply indents to paragraphs in a letter.

Files needed: Chapter 4 Time Out Letter.docx, open from the preceding exercise

1. **In the Chapter 4 Time Out Letter document, triple-click the paragraph containing the quotation to select it (the paragraph that begins with "***I really enjoy . . .***").**

2. **Choose Home⇨Increase Indent.**

   The left indent increases by 0.5 inch. See Figure 4-9.

Increase Indent button

Increased left indent

Figure 4-9

3. **Click the dialog box launcher in the Paragraph group to open the Paragraph dialog box.**

4. **Click the up arrow on the Right text box to increase the right indent to 0.5 inch (see Figure 4-10) and then click OK.**

   The paragraph is indented 0.5 inch on each side.

Right indent increased to 0.5"

Figure 4-10

5. **Click in the paragraph that begins *"Our sales . . ."* and then click the dialog box launcher again to reopen the Paragraph dialog box.**

6. **From the Special drop-down list, choose First Line.**

   A first-line indent default value of 0.5 inch appears. See Figure 4-11.

7. **Click OK.**

   That paragraph is now first-line indented by 0.5 inch.

First line indent set to 0.5"

Figure 4-11

EXTRA INFO

You can also create a first-line indent by positioning the insertion point at the beginning of a paragraph and pressing the Tab key. Typically this would place a 0.5-inch tab at the beginning of the paragraph, but Word's AutoCorrect feature immediately converts it to a real first-line indent for you.

For more practice, try setting a hanging indent for one of the remaining paragraphs. Choose Hanging from the Special drop-down list in the Paragraph dialog box. When you're finished, press Ctrl+Z to undo.

8. **Save the changes to the document and close it.**

Leave Word open for the next exercise.

Adjusting indents with the Ruler

If the Ruler is displayed in Word, you can see indent markers on it showing where the current paragraph is indented. Choose View⇨Ruler to toggle the Ruler on or off.

If no indents are applied, the indent markers coincide with the margins. The margins are represented on the Ruler by the areas where the Ruler's color changes from dark gray to light gray.

The indent markers are as follows:

- ✔ **Down-pointing triangle at the left:** First-line indent. Drag this triangle to adjust the indent of the first line only.

- ✔ **Up-pointing triangle at the left:** Subsequent-lines indent. Drag this triangle to adjust the indent of all lines except the first one.

- ✔ **Rectangle at the left:** Left indent. Drag this rectangle to adjust the overall left indent for the paragraph. If the triangles at the left are not both at the same position, dragging the rectangle will adjust the left indent proportionally, keeping the current relationship between the two.

- ✔ **Up-pointing triangle at the right:** Right indent. Drag this triangle to adjust the right indent. You can't adjust the right indent for different lines in the same paragraph separately.

Figure 4-12 shows the indent markers on the Ruler for a paragraph that's indented 1 inch at both left and right margins and the first line is indented an additional 0.5 inch.

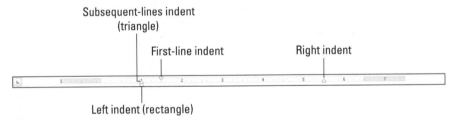

Figure 4-12

In the following exercise, you adjust indents using the Ruler.

Files needed: Chapter 4 Time Out Letter.docx

1. **In Chapter 4 Time Out Letter, click in the quotation paragraph.**

   The indent markers for that paragraph appear on the Ruler. If the Ruler doesn't appear, select the Ruler check box on the View tab.

2. **Drag the left indent marker (the rectangle at the left) to the 1" mark on the Ruler.**

   Be careful that you drag the rectangle, not one of the triangles.

3. **Drag the right indent marker (the triangle at the right) to the 5.5" mark on the Ruler (see Figure 4-13).**

Set the Left indent to 1"   Set the Right indent to 5.5"

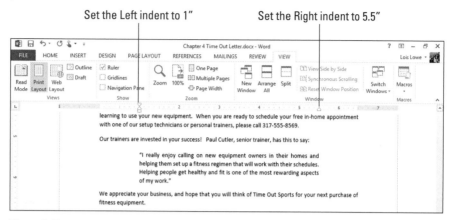

Figure 4-13

4. Click in the paragraph that begins *"Our sales and support . . ."*

Note that the two triangles on the left end of the Ruler are not aligned with one another; the first-line indent is set at 0.5".

5. Drag the first-line indent (the upper triangle) to the left margin (0" on the Ruler).

The first-line indent is removed from the paragraph.

6. Save and close the document.

Leave Word open for the next exercise.

Setting Tab Stops

Tab stops are position markers in a paragraph that specify where the insertion point will move when you press the Tab key. By default, a paragraph has tab stops every 0.5 inch, but you can change to some other interval or create custom tab stops.

Tab stops can have different alignments. Figure 4-14 shows the different ways tab stops can align columns of text, and the associated tab stop symbols on the Ruler. Table 4-1 takes a closer look at the different types of tab stops.

LINGO

Tab stops are position markers in a paragraph that specify where the insertion point will move when you press the Tab key.

Figure 4-14

Table 4-1	Aligning Columns of Text with Tab Stops	
Tab Stop Alignment	**Looks Like**	**How It Works**
Left (default)	The letter L	After you press Tab, begins text at the tab stop position
Right	A backward L	Moves text over so that its end aligns with the tab stop
Center	An upside-down T	Centers the text from the tab stop position
Decimal	An upside-down T with a black dot in its lower-right corner	Aligns numbers so that their decimal points are at the tab stop position

A *tab leader* is a character that repeats to form a line that helps guide the reader's eye across the page. Any tab stop can have a leader applied to it. The leader fills in the space between that tab and the preceding one with the leader character. For example, in Figure 4-15, a leader has been applied to the tab stop at the 6" position on the Ruler.

LINGO

A **tab leader** repeats to form a line that guides the reader's eye across the page.

Right tab stop

Leader

Figure 4-15

Creating tab stops

You can create tab stops with the Ruler or with the Tabs dialog box. The following exercise shows both methods.

In the following exercise, you create tab stops and then use them to create a multicolumn list.

Files needed: None

1. **In Word, press Ctrl+N to start a new blank document and then press the Tab key several times.**

   Notice that the insertion point moves 0.5" to the right each time you press Tab. That's because the default tab stops are at 0.5" intervals.

2. **Press the Backspace key until the insertion point returns to the left margin, removing all the tabs you typed.**

3. **On the Home tab, click the dialog box launcher in the Paragraph group to open the Paragraph dialog box and then click the Tabs button.**

   The Tabs dialog box opens.

4. **In the Default Tab Stops box, click the up arrow until the setting is 1".**

   Default tab stops are now at 1" intervals.

5. **In the Tab Stop Position box, type 5"; in the Alignment area, click Right; in the Leader area, click 2 (the dotted line); and then click Set.**

The new tab stop appears on the list below the Tab Stop Position box. See Figure 4-16.

6. **Click OK to close the dialog box.**

7. **Type** Chapter 1 **and press the Tab key once.**

The insertion point moves to the 5" tab stop.

8. **Type** 1 **and then press Enter.**

The new paragraph has the same tab stops as the preceding one unless you change them.

9. **Choose Home⇨Clear All Formatting.**

The right-aligned tab stop at 5" is removed from the new paragraph, leaving only the default tab stops.

10. **Press the Tab key twice.**

Notice that the insertion point moves 1" each time you press Tab because you redefined the default tab stops in Step 4.

Use a leader.

Create a tab stop at 5".

Right-align the tab stop.

Figure 4-16

11. **Press the Backspace key twice to remove the two tabs you typed and then click the Tab Type button at the far left of the Ruler until the tab type is center (an upside-down T — the plain one, not the one with the dot on its right side).**

12. **Click the Ruler at the 2.5" mark to set a center-aligned tab stop there and then press the Tab key once to move the insertion point to the new tab stop.**

13. **Type** Note: Page numbers are preliminary.

The text you type center-aligns with the tab stop. See Figure 4-17.

14. **Save the document as Chapter 4 Tabs.**

Leave the document open for the next exercise.

EXTRA INFO

The Tab Type button toggles among several tab and other settings. If you accidentally click past the center tab stop type, keep clicking and it will come back around again.

Center-aligned tab stop

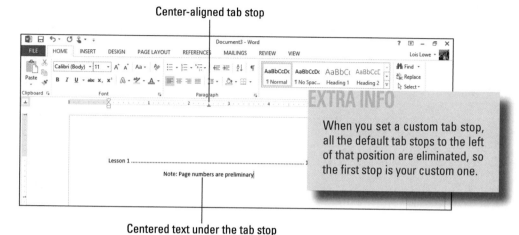

EXTRA INFO

When you set a custom tab stop, all the default tab stops to the left of that position are eliminated, so the first stop is your custom one.

Lesson 1 1

Note: Page numbers are preliminary

Centered text under the tab stop

Figure 4-17

Changing and removing tab stops

The easiest way to change and remove tab stops is to work with them directly on the Ruler. You can drag a tab stop to the right or left to shift its position, or you can drag it off the Ruler entirely (up or down) to remove it.

To change a tab stop's type, double-click the tab stop on the Ruler to open the Tabs dialog box and make your changes there.

In the following exercise, you modify and remove tab stops.

Files needed: Chapter 4 Tabs.docx, open from the preceding exercise

1. **In the Chapter 4 Tabs document, click in the paragraph that begins with "Note . . ."**

   The Ruler shows one custom tab stop for that paragraph: a center-aligned tab at the 2.5" mark.

2. **Drag the tab stop down off the Ruler to delete it.**

   The text reverts to left-aligned with the default tab stop at the 1" mark.

When no custom tab stops are set for a paragraph, the paragraph reverts to the default tab stops. This paragraph has default tab stops every 1" because in an earlier exercise, you changed the default from its original 0.5" setting.

3. **Click in the Chapter 1 paragraph.**

The Ruler shows a custom tab stop at the 5" mark.

4. **Drag the custom tab stop from the 5" mark to the 6" mark on the Ruler.**

The number 1 moves to the 6" mark on the Ruler, and the leader extends to fill the extra space. See Figure 4-18.

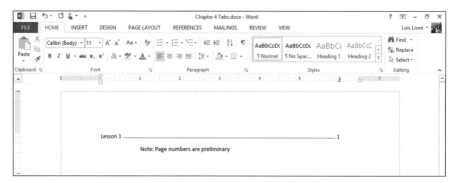

Figure 4-18

5. **Save the document and close it.**

Leave Word open for the next exercise.

Creating Bulleted and Numbered Lists

Word makes it easy to create bulleted and numbered lists in your documents:

✔ **Use a bulleted list when the order of list items isn't significant.** The same bullet character (such as •) is used in front of each item. You might use a bulleted list for a packing list for a trip, for example, or a go-forward list.

✔ **Use a numbered list when the order of list items *is* significant and a sequential step number is used to indicate order.** For example, a numbered list might contain the steps for a recipe or a meeting agenda.

You can create a list from existing paragraphs, or you can turn on the list feature and type the list as you go. Either way, you're working with the Bullets button or the Numbering button on the Home tab.

In the following exercise, you convert some paragraphs into a numbered list and then change it to a bulleted list.

Files needed: Chapter 4 Time Out Letter.docx

1. **Open the Chapter 4 Time Out Letter file, created earlier in this chapter.**

2. **Select the list of four benefits, starting with** *"Free in-home setup . . ."* **and then choose Home⇨Numbering.**

   The list becomes numbered.

3. **Click the Bullets button.**

   The list switches to a bulleted list. See Figure 4-19.

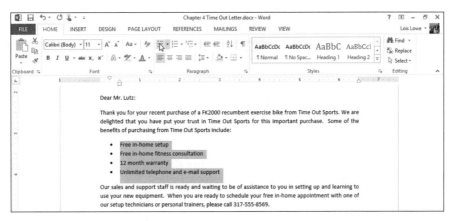

Figure 4-19

Leave the document open for the next exercise.

Changing the bullet character

You can use any character you like for the bullets in a bulleted list; you're not limited to the standard black circle. Word offers a choice of several common characters on a palette accessible via the Bullets button, and you can also select any picture or character from any font to use.

In the following exercise, you change the bullet character to several that are text-based or graphical.

Files needed: Chapter 4 Time Out Letter.docx, open from the preceding exercise

1. In the Chapter 4 Time Out Letter document, select the four bulleted paragraphs.

2. From the Home tab, click the down arrow on the Bullets button, opening its palette (see Figure 4-20), and then choose the check mark bullet.

The list uses that character.

Figure 4-20

3. Click the down arrow on the Bullets button again, reopening its palette, and choose Define New Bullet.

The Define New Bullet dialog box opens.

4. Click the Symbol button to open the Symbol dialog box.

5. From the Font drop-down list, choose Wingdings if it's not already selected (see Figure 4-21).

Figure 4-21

6. Click the six-pointed black star (scroll if needed to find it), click OK to close the Symbol dialog box, and then click OK to close the Define New Bullet dialog box.

The bulleted list appears with the new star bullets.

7. **Click the down arrow on the Bullets button again, reopening its palette, and then choose Define New Bullet.**

   The Define New Bullet dialog box opens.

8. **Click the Picture button.**

   The Insert Pictures dialog box opens. See Figure 4-22.

Figure 4-22

9. **Click in the Office.com Clip Art text box and type** bullet, **and then press Enter.**

10. **Click any of the picture bullets that appeal to you and then click Insert.**

    Choose one of the simple graphics, not one of the photos of gun bullets.

11. **Click OK to close the Define New Bullet dialog box.**

    The picture bullets appear in the document.

12. **Save the changes to the document.**

Leave the document open for the next exercise.

Changing the numbering style

Changing the numbering style is much like changing the bullet character, except you have a few extra options, such as choosing a starting number. You can select from various styles of numbering that include uppercase or lowercase letters, Roman numerals, or Arabic (regular) numerals.

In the following exercise, you change the numbering format for a numbered list.

Files needed: Chapter 4 Time Out Letter.docx, open from the preceding exercise

1. In the Chapter 4 Time Out Letter document, select the four bulleted paragraphs if they aren't already selected.

2. From the Home tab, click the down arrow on the Numbering button to open its palette.

3. In the Numbering Library section, choose the numbering style that uses uppercase letters followed by periods (see Figure 4-23).

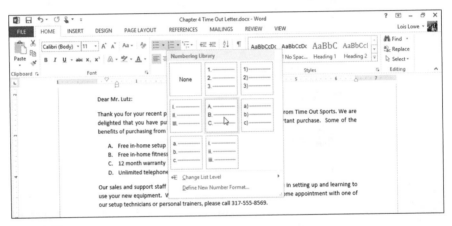

Figure 4-23

4. Click the down arrow on the Numbering button and then choose Define New Number Format.

   The Define New Number Format dialog box appears.

5. In the Number Format text box, delete the period following the shaded A and type a colon (:), as shown in Figure 4-24.

6. Click the Font button to open the Font dialog box, set the font size to 14 points (see Figure 4-25), click OK to return to the Define New Number Format dialog box, and then click OK to accept the new format.

Figure 4-24

Figure 4-25

Note: The black-filled check boxes in the Effects section of the Font dialog box mean the attributes will be left at their current settings, and not specified one way or another by the number format being defined.

The list appears with extra-large letters, followed by colons. See Figure 4-26.

7. Save the changes to the document.

Leave the document open for the next exercise.

A:	Free in-home setup
B:	Free in-home fitness consultation
C:	12 month warranty
D:	Unlimited telephone and e-mail support

Figure 4-26

Adding Borders and Shading

By default, a paragraph has no border or shading. You can add either or both to a single paragraph or any group of paragraphs to make them stand out from the rest of the document. You can use any border thickness, style, and color you like, and any color of shading.

Placing a border around a paragraph

A paragraph border appears around the outside of a single paragraph. If the paragraph is indented, the border will also be indented (left and right only; the indent doesn't change for hanging or first-line indents).

If you place the same border around two or more consecutive paragraphs, the border surrounds them as a group. That way, you can create groups of paragraphs that appear boxed together for special emphasis.

In the following exercise, you add a border around a paragraph.

Files needed: Chapter 4 Time Out Letter.docx, open from the preceding exercise

1. **In the Chapter 4 Time Out Letter document, click anywhere within the quotation paragraph.**

2. **On the Home tab, in the Paragraph group, open the Borders button's drop-down list and choose Outside Borders.**

   A plain black border appears around the quotation paragraph. See Figure 4-27. You can stop here if you want a plain border, but the next steps show you how to format the border in different ways.

Figure 4-27

3. **From the Border button's drop-down list, choose Borders and Shading.**

   The Borders and Shading dialog box opens.

4. **Click the Shadow button.**

   The border becomes thicker at the bottom and right sides, simulating a shadow.

 Check the results in the preview in the dialog box.

5. **Click the Box button.**

   The border once again has the same thickness on all sides. Check the results in the preview.

6. **From the Color drop-down list, choose the Blue, Accent 1 theme color; from the Width drop-down list, choose ½ pt; in the Style area, click one of the dashed lines; and in the Preview area, click the buttons that represent the right and left sides, turning off those sides (see Figure 4-28).**

Turn off the borders on the sides

Figure 4-28

7. **Click OK to apply the border to the paragraph and then save the document.**

Leave the document open for the next exercise.

Shading a paragraph's background

Shading a paragraph helps it stand out from the rest of the document and adds visual interest. You can use shading with or without a border.

As with a border, shading follows along with any indent settings you may have specified for the paragraph. If the paragraph is indented, the shading is also.

TIP

Word applies only solid-color shading to paragraphs. If you want a gradient shading behind a paragraph, or some other special shading effect such as a pattern, texture, or graphic, place a text box (choose Insert⇨Text Box) and then apply the desired shading to the text box as a Fill, like you would with a graphic. Then type the desired text into the text box. See Chapter 8 for more information.

In the following exercise, you add shading to a paragraph.

Files needed: Chapter 4 Time Out Letter.docx, open from the preceding exercise

1. **In the Chapter 4 Time Out Letter document, click anywhere within the quotation paragraph.**

2. **On the Home tab, in the Paragraph group, open the Shading drop-down list and choose Blue, Accent 1, Lighter 80%, as shown in Figure 4-29.**

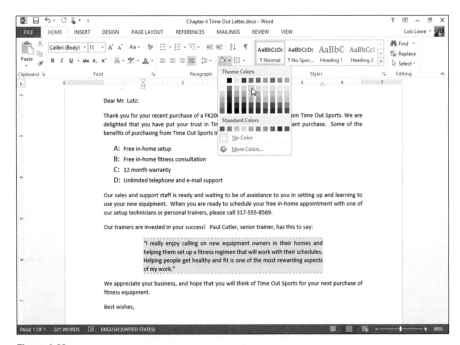

Figure 4-29

3. **Reopen the Shading drop-down list and choose More Colors.**

   The Colors dialog box opens.

4. **Click the Standard tab, click a light yellow square (see Figure 4-30), and then click OK to accept the new color choice.**

5. **Save and close the document.**

Exit Word.

Figure 4-30

 Summing Up

Word provides several ways to format paragraphs and tables and to help automate formatting. Here are the key points from this chapter:

- To apply horizontal alignment, use the buttons in the Paragraph group on the Home tab. Your choices are Align Text Left, Align Text Right, Center, and Justify.

- You can set line and paragraph spacing from the Paragraph dialog box.

- A paragraph can be indented at the left or right (all lines) and can have a first-line or hanging indent applied.

- To indent the entire paragraph at the left, you can use the Increase Indent button in the Paragraph group on the Home tab.

- To set other indentation, open the Paragraph dialog box by clicking the dialog box launcher in the Paragraph group.

- To set tab stops, click the Ruler. To remove tab stops, drag them off the Ruler. You can also work with tab stops in the Tabs dialog box, accessed from the Paragraph dialog box.

- To create a default numbered or bulleted list, use their respective buttons on the Home tab. Each button has a drop-down list from which you can choose other bullet or numbering styles.

- To add a border to a paragraph, use the Border button's drop-down list on the Home tab.

- To add shading to a paragraph, use the Shading button's drop-down list on the Home tab.

Try-it-yourself lab

For more practice with the features covered in this chapter, try the following exercise on your own:

1. **In a new document, type** Shopping List **and then center the paragraph.**
2. **Place a border and shading around the Shopping List text.**
3. **Below that paragraph, create a bulleted list consisting of at least eight items you'd buy at a grocery store.**
4. **Indent the paragraphs of the bulleted list by 0.5" more than its default.**
5. **Save your document with a name of your choice and close Word.**

Know this tech talk

border: An outline around an object.

bulleted list: A list in which each paragraph is preceded by the same symbol.

first-line indent: A positive indent that affects only the first line of the paragraph. When negative, it's a *hanging indent*.

hanging indent: A negative indent that affects only the first line of the paragraph. When positive, it's a *first-line indent*.

horizontal alignment: The positioning of a paragraph between the right and left margins.

indentation: The amount that a paragraph is offset from the left or right margin.

justified: A horizontal alignment that stretches out the text so that it touches both the right and left margins.

leading: Spacing between the lines of text.

numbered list: A list in which each paragraph is preceded by a consecutive number.

paragraph formatting: Formatting that affects whole paragraphs and cannot be applied to individual characters.

shading: The background fill in a paragraph or object.

tab stop: A position marker for a paragraph that indicates where the insertion point should move when the Tab key is pressed.

Chapter 5

Standardizing Formatting with Styles and Templates

- Styles *make consistent formatting quick and easy to apply*.

- You can create your own styles to consistently *apply your own custom formatting*.

- The Style Inspector enables you to *see exactly what formatting has been applied* to selected text.

- You can modify templates to *create your own custom versions* of the templates that come with Word.

Styles and templates simplify document formatting and help you format your documents consistently.

A *style* contains a set of formatting commands for an individual paragraph, list item, or character of text. When a style holds a set of formatting instructions, you can apply all that style's formatting with a single click. Templates can store styles so that when you start a document with a certain template, that set of styles is automatically available to you.

A *template* is a sample that you can base new documents on; it can contain sample content, styles, margin settings, and other formatting that jump-starts the document creation.

In this chapter, you learn how to apply styles, modify existing style definitions, and create new ones. You also learn how to modify a template and how to create your own templates.

Simplifying Formatting with Preset Styles

Using a style makes it easy to apply consistent formatting throughout a document. For example, you might apply the Heading 1 style to all headings in the document and the Normal style to all the regular body text. Here are the advantages of this approach:

- ✔ **Ease:** Applying a style is easier than manually applying formatting. And changing the formatting is a snap. If you want the headings to look different, for example, you can modify the Heading 1 style to change them all at once.

- ✔ **Consistency:** You don't have to worry about all the headings being formatted consistently; because they're all using the same style, they're automatically all the same.

By default, each paragraph is assigned a Normal style. The template in use determines the styles available and how they're defined.

TIP

In Word 2013 documents that use the default blank (Normal) template, the Normal style uses Calibri 11-point font and left-aligns the text, with no indentation.

You can redefine the styles in a document and create your own new styles.

Applying a style

The Normal template, on which new blank documents are based in Word, contains some basic styles you can use to get started, such as Heading 1, Heading 2, and Normal. To see what styles are available in your current template, start on the Home tab, where you find a Styles gallery. The first row appears on the Ribbon itself, and you can see the rest of it by clicking the More button to open the full gallery.

LINGO

The **Styles gallery** on the Home tab contains shortcuts for commonly used styles.

REMEMBER

Not all styles appear in the Styles gallery — only the ones designated to appear there in their definition. The rest of them appear only in the Styles pane. To open the Styles pane, click the dialog box launcher on the Styles group.

To apply a style, select the paragraph(s) that you want to affect, or move the insertion point into the paragraph. Then click the style you want to apply, either in the Styles gallery or in the Styles pane. If a keyboard shortcut is assigned to a style, you press the keyboard shortcut to apply the style, too.

In the following exercise, you apply styles to the paragraphs in a document.

Files needed: Chapter 5 Syllabus.docx

1. **In Word, open Chapter 5 Syllabus and save it as Chapter 5 Syllabus Formatted.**

2. **Click in the first paragraph *(CIT 233)*. Then on the Home tab, in the Styles group, click the More button (see Figure 5-1) to open the Styles gallery.**

More button

Figure 5-1

3. **Click the Title style (see Figure 5-2).**

   The style is applied to the first paragraph.

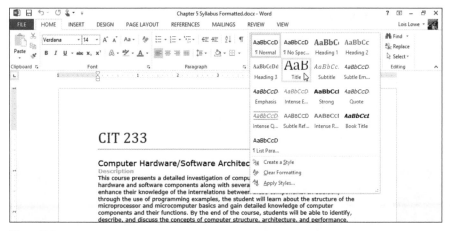

Figure 5-2

4. **Using the same procedure as Steps 2 through 3, apply the Subtitle style to the second paragraph.**

5. **Apply the Heading 1 style to each of the orange paragraphs by clicking Heading 1 in the Style gallery.**

   TIP

   Here's a shortcut: Click to the left of the first orange paragraph to select it, and then hold down the Ctrl key and do the same for each of the remaining orange paragraphs. After they're all selected, apply the style to them all at once.

6. **Click the dialog box launcher in the Styles group to open the Styles pane.**

7. **Scroll through the Styles pane and locate the Heading 2 style; then click in one of the green paragraphs near the end of the document and click the Heading 2 style in the Styles pane to apply it.**

8. **Apply the Heading 2 style to all the remaining green paragraphs.**

   The last page of the document resembles Figure 5-3.

EXTRA INFO

Scroll through the Styles pane's list, and look at the symbols to the right of each style. Most of the styles in the Styles pane have a paragraph symbol (¶) to their right. This means that they are *paragraph styles* — they apply to entire paragraphs at once. They may include both paragraph and character formatting in their definitions, but if you click in a paragraph and then apply the style, the style will be applied to the whole paragraph. In contrast, some styles may have a lowercase *a* to their right on the list; these are *character styles,* or *text-level styles,* and they apply only to the text that you select before applying them. A character style can contain only character-based formatting.

Visit this website to learn more about resources here on campus and how to define research article materials: http://inflite.ulib.iupui.edu/
Do you truly understand plagiarism? Go to this website and go through the tutorial to find out: http://tutorials.sjlibrary.org/plagiarism/index.htm

Resources Available

Writing Assistance
A written research paper is required for this class. If you would like help with any of your academic writing assignments, visit the TCM Writing Center in ET 314-A. The Writing Center offers free tutoring to all IUPUI students. I encourage you to use the Center's services. If you have questions about the services the Center offers or just want more information, call 317-555-1311.

Adaptive Services
If you need any adaptive educational services, please don't hesitate to contact your instructor. Being notified of any needs early in the semester will help to ensure your success in the class. Services are also provided by AES (Adaptive Educational Services) and can be reached via their website at http://life.iupui.edu/aes/ , by calling 317-555-3241.

Figure 5-3

9. **Save the changes to the document.**

Leave the document open for the next exercise.

Modifying a style

You can modify a style in two ways: by example or by manually changing the style's definition. The by-example method is much easier, but somewhat less flexible. The following exercise shows both methods.

In the following exercise, you change the definitions of some styles.

Files needed: Chapter 5 Syllabus Formatted.docx, open from the preceding exercise

1. **Triple-click the document sub-title (the second paragraph) to select it and then change the font size to 18 points.**

2. **In the Styles pane, click the down arrow to the right of the Subtitle style, or right-click the Subtitle style.**

3. **In the menu that appears, choose Update Subtitle to Match Selection, as shown in Figure 5-4.**

   The style is updated with the new font size.

4. **Reopen the Subtitle style's menu and choose Modify.**

   The Modify Style dialog box opens.

Figure 5-4

For more practice, make other changes to the style's definition using the font controls in the Modify Style dialog box. The buttons and lists in the dialog box correspond to the tools in the Font and Paragraph groups on the Home tab.

5. **In the bottom-left corner of the dialog box, click the Format button and choose Font (see Figure 5-5) to open the Font dialog box.**

Figure 5-5

6. **Select the Small Caps check box, as shown in Figure 5-6, and then click OK to return to the Modify Style dialog box.**

Notice the Add to the Styles Gallery check box in the bottom-left corner of the Modify Style dialog box. This check box's status is what determines whether a particular style appears in the Styles gallery on the Ribbon.

7. **Click OK to close the Modify Style dialog box.**

The style definition is updated.

8. **Save the changes to the document.**

Leave the document open for the next exercise.

Because the Subtitle style is used only once in this document, you don't get to see one of the biggest benefits of styles in this exercise: the fact that when you update a style, all text that has that style applied to it updates automatically. For more practice, change the definition of the Heading 1 or Heading 2 style, and watch all the instances change.

Figure 5-6

Creating a new style

The built-in styles are a nice start, but creating your own styles is where the magic happens. Creating styles is especially useful if you want to build a template that you can give to other people to make sure that everyone formats documents the same way, such as in a group in which each person assembles a different section of a report.

When you create your own styles, you can name them anything you like. Most people like to name styles based on their purposes, to make it easier to choose which style to apply. For example, *Figure Caption* would be a good name — *Style13* would not.

Just like when modifying a style, you can create a new style either by example or by manually specifying a style definition.

If you go with the definition method, you can specify some additional options that aren't available with the by-example method, such as defining which style follows this style. In other words, if someone types a paragraph using this style and then presses Enter, what style will the next new paragraph be? The paragraph that follows a heading style is usually a body paragraph style. The paragraph that follows a body paragraph is usually another body paragraph.

Each new style is based on an existing style (usually the Normal style) so that if there's a particular formatting aspect you don't specify, it trickles down from the parent style. For example, suppose you create a new style dubbed Important, and you base it on the Normal style. The Important style starts out with identical formatting to the Normal style, which is Calibri 11-point font. You might then modify it to have bold, red text. The definition of Important is Normal+bold+red. That's significant if you later change the definition of Normal to 12-point font. That font size change trickles down to Important automatically, and all text formatted with the Important style becomes 12 points in size.

In the following exercise, you create a new style.

Files needed: Chapter 5 Syllabus Formatted.docx, open from the preceding exercise

1. **Triple-click the first bulleted item** *(CPUs and Assembly language)* **to select it.**

2. **At the bottom of the Styles pane, click the New Style button.**

   The Create New Style from Formatting dialog box opens (see Figure 5-7).

3. **In the Name box, type** Bulleted List, **and then click the Format button in the lower-left corner of the dialog box and choose Numbering.**

   The Numbering and Bullets dialog box appears.

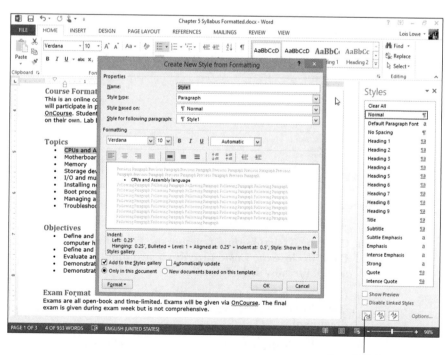

New Style button

Figure 5-7

4. Click the Bullets tab (see Figure 5-8), click the white circle bullet character, and then click OK.

5. Click the Format button again and choose Shortcut Key.

   The Customize Keyboard dialog box opens.

6. Press Ctrl+Q.

   That key combination appears in the Press New Shortcut Key box.

7. Open the Save Changes In drop-down list and choose Chapter 5 Syllabus Formatted.docx, as shown in Figure 5-9.

Figure 5-8

Figure 5-9

8. Click the Assign button to assign the keyboard shortcut to the style, click Close to close the Customize Keyboard dialog box, and then click OK to accept the new style definition.

9. Using any method (for example, the Ctrl+Q shortcut), apply the new style, Bulleted List, to all the remaining bulleted paragraphs in the document.

10. Save the changes to the document and close it.

Leave Word open for the next exercise.

Importing styles from other documents

Each document stores its own styles. These styles originate from the template on which the document is based, but ultimately each document's styles are its own. So, for example, if you make a change to a style's definition in one document, or create new styles in that document, those changes and new styles will not be available in any other documents.

To save yourself the time and effort of re-creating new styles that you want to use in both documents, you can import styles from one document into another one.

You can start in either document — the styles' source or their destination — but the process is shorter by a few steps if you start in the source document.

In the following exercise, you copy styles from one document to another.

Files needed: Chapter 5 Styles.docx and Chapter 5 Syllabus Formatted.docx

1. **Open Chapter 5 Styles.**

   This document contains three new styles: Report Heading 1, Report Heading 2, and Report Heading 3.

You don't need to save Chapter 5 Styles with a different name because you don't modify it in this exercise.

2. **On the Home tab, click the dialog box launcher in the Styles group to open the Styles pane and then click the Manage Styles button at the bottom (see Figure 5-10).**

   The Manage Styles dialog box opens.

3. **At the bottom of the Manage Styles dialog box, click the Import/ Export button.**

   The Organizer dialog box opens.

4. **Click the Close File button on the right (under Normal.dotm) and then click the Open File button.**

   The Open dialog box appears.

5. **Click All Word Templates, which opens a list of file types, and choose All Word Documents from the list (see Figure 5-11).**

Dialog box launcher for the
Styles group

Import/Export button   Manage Styles button

Figure 5-10

Set the file type to All Word Documents.

Figure 5-11

6. **Navigate to the folder where you stored the file Chapter 5 Syllabus Formatted, select that file, and click Open.**

   A list of the styles in that document appears in the right pane. See Figure 5-12.

Figure 5-12

7. **Click Report Heading 1 in the left pane. Press the Shift key and click Report Heading 3.**

   All three custom styles are selected.

8. **Click the Copy button.**

   Those styles are copied to Chapter 5 Syllabus Formatted in the right pane.

9. **In the right pane, scroll down to confirm that the new styles appear on the list and then click Close.**

10. **If you see a prompt asking whether you want to save the changes to Chapter 5 Syllabus Formatted, click Save.**

    The styles are saved.

11. **Close Chapter 5 Styles without saving the changes.**

12. **Open Chapter 5 Syllabus Formatted, and on the Home tab, click the dialog box launcher in the Styles group, opening the Styles pane.**

13. **Scroll through the list of styles and locate the three newly copied styles (see Figure 5-13).**

Leave the document open for the next exercise.

Seeing what styles are applied

Word offers a few ways to see what styles are applied to a paragraph or text:

- ✔ **Styles gallery:** Use this method when you need to see the style applied to a single paragraph at a glance. You have been working with the Styles gallery throughout this chapter.

- ✔ **Styles area pane in Draft and Outline views:** This method enables you to check what styles are applied to each paragraph as you scroll through your document.

- ✔ **Style Inspector:** This dialog box enables you to do sophisticated sleuthing into the styles applied to each paragraph.

Styles	▾ ✕
Bulleted List	¶
Normal	¶
Report Heading 1	¶
Report Heading 2	¶
Report Heading 3	¶
Default Paragraph Font	a
No Spacing	¶
Heading 1	¶a
Heading 2	¶a
Heading 3	¶a
Heading 4	¶a
Heading 5	¶a
Heading 6	¶a
Heading 7	¶a
Heading 8	¶a
Heading 9	¶a
Title	¶a
Subtitle	¶a
Subtle Emphasis	a
Emphasis	a
Intense Emphasis	a

☐ Show Preview
☐ Disable Linked Styles

Options...

— Newly copied styles

Figure 5-13

To check what style is applied to every paragraph, display the Styles area pane in Draft or Outline view. To do so, choose File⇨Options. In the Word Options dialog box, click Advanced, and then scroll down to the Display section, and in the box labeled Style Area Pane Width in Draft and Outline Views, type a width, such as 0.5", and click OK. Now in Draft view, you see each style applied along the left side of the screen.

The Style Inspector enables you to click around to see each paragraph's style, but its real power lies in the Reveal Formatting feature. With the Reveal Formatting pane displayed, you can

- ✔ See all the formatting bundled into a single style.

- ✔ Compare styles to see exactly how one style differs from another.

TIP

You'll probably find the Style Inspector most useful when you're trying to troubleshoot a problem with one or more styles. For example, Reveal Formatting can show a formatting rule that unintentionally strayed into a style. Or if the spacing before and after headings doesn't look consistent, the compare feature can tell you exactly how the Heading 1 and Heading 2 styles are different. Then you can see at a glance how you need to modify your heading styles.

The Style Inspector is handy for examining the formatting that's applied to text. For example, you can see at a glance whether additional manual formatting has been applied to the text in addition to the formatting it receives from the style applied to it. You can also use the Style Inspector to quickly strip all the character or paragraph formatting from the text.

LINGO

The **Style Inspector** is a floating pane you can enable that shows what paragraph-level and text-level formatting is applied to the selected text.

In the following exercise, you use the Style Inspector to check the formatting on some text.

Files needed: Chapter 5 Syllabus Formatted.docx, open from the preceding exercise

1. **If the Styles pane is not already visible, on the Home tab, click the dialog box launcher in the Styles group to display it.**

2. **At the bottom of the Styles pane, click the Style Inspector button.**

   The Style Inspector pane opens. See Figure 5-14.

3. **Click in the *CIT 233* paragraph if the insertion point is not already there.**

   The Style Inspector shows that the paragraph formatting is the Title style and the text-level formatting is the default paragraph font with no additional formatting, as shown in Figure 5-14.

4. **Press the down-arrow key once to move the insertion point to the next paragraph.**

   Its information appears in the Style Inspector window. See Figure 5-15.

Figure 5-14

5. **Click the Reveal Formatting button at the bottom of the Style Inspector pane.**

A Reveal Formatting pane appears, showing details about the formatting of the text where the insertion point currently rests. See Figure 5-16.

6. **Triple-click the paragraph to select all the text in it and then change the font size to 12.**

7. **Look in the Reveal Formatting task pane at the font size, which shows 12 points.**

8. **In the Style Inspector, click the Clear Character Formatting button.**

Figure 5-15

The manually applied character formatting is removed, leaving only the formatting from the style. The font size changes because the definition of the Subtitle style calls for 18-point font. See Figure 5-17.

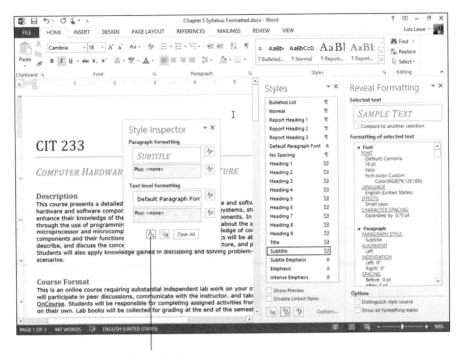

Reveal Formatting button

Figure 5-16

9. **In the Style Inspector pane, click the Reset to Normal Paragraph Style button.**

   The Subtitle style is removed from the selected text, and the text appears using Normal style.

10. **Press Ctrl+Z or click the Undo button on the Quick Access Toolbar to reverse the last action.**

11. **Close the Style Inspector, Styles, and Reveal Formatting panes.**

12. **Save the document and close it.**

Leave Word open for the next exercise.

Figure 5-17

Changing and Creating Templates

Every document has a template that it references. The template provides such basics as the margin settings and the definition of the Normal paragraph style. The template also may provide a list of styles. In addition, some templates provide sample content, including text, graphics, text boxes, and hyperlinks.

LINGO

A **template** is a special type of document that stores formatting settings and boilerplate text on which you can base new documents.

Many templates are available via Office.com; you can select one by choosing File⇨New and then browsing the list. (Chapter 2 explains the process in detail.) You can also customize templates to meet your own needs and even create your own templates. That's what this section is all about.

Template files use a .dotx extension, rather than the regular .docx for documents. Word 2013 can also use templates from Word 2003 and earlier, which have .dot extensions, and macro-enabled templates, which have .dotm extensions.

Modifying an existing template

Templates provide great shortcuts to document formatting, but if a template isn't exactly what you want it to be, you waste time each time you use it, making the same modifications over and over. For example, perhaps you find yourself changing the colors each time or filling in the same placeholders with your company's data. It is often easier to make changes to the template itself once.

In this exercise, you open a template and make changes to it, and then save the changes and start a new document based upon it.

Files needed: Chapter 5 Certificate.dotx

1. **Open the template Chapter 5 Certificate.**

   Don't just start a new document based upon it, but open the template itself. To do so:

   a. Choose File⇨Open and then navigate to the folder containing the data files for this chapter.

   b. In the Open dialog box, click All Word Documents and then choose All Word Templates to limit the list of files to those with a template extension (.dotx). See Figure 5-18.

   c. Click Chapter 5 Certificate.dotx and then click Open.

   The template opens for editing.

2. **Choose File⇨Options, click Save, and note the location in the Default Personal Templates Location text box; see Figure 5-19. Then click OK to close the dialog box.**

Set the file type to All Word Templates.

Figure 5-18

Note the location for your personal templates;
enter a location here if none exists.

Figure 5-19

Note: If no entry is in the Default Personal Templates Location text box, enter a location that you would like to use for your templates. For example, you might create a Custom Templates folder in your Documents folder for this purpose. You won't be able to access your saved templates unless a location is listed in this text box.

3. **Save the template file as Chapter 5 Certificate Template, in the location you noted in Step 2.**

4. **Triple-click the *[Your Jr. High School]* placeholder to select it and then type** Dayton Junior High School.

5. **Save the template and close it.**

6. **Choose File⇨New and then click the Personal heading (see Figure 5-20). Then click the Chapter 5 Certificate Template.**

   A new document opens that uses the customized version of the template.

   Note: if the Personal heading does not appear, go back to Step 2 and make sure you set a location in the Word Options dialog box for your personal templates.

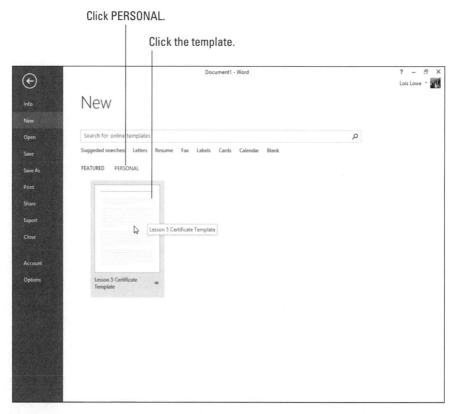

Figure 5-20

7. Close the new document without saving the changes to it.

Leave Word open for the next exercise.

Creating a new template

You can create your own templates whenever you like. These might contain sample content you've created, plus special margin settings, extra styles, or anything else that you want to reuse.

In this exercise, you create a new template with custom margin settings and a custom header.

Files needed: None

1. Press Ctrl+N to start a new document based on the Normal template (a blank document with default settings).

2. Choose Page Layout⇨Margins⇨ Moderate to change the document margins (see Figure 5-21).

3. Choose Design⇨Page Color and select Blue, Accent 1, Lighter 80% (see Figure 5-22).

4. Choose Insert⇨Header⇨ Motion (Even Page), shown in Figure 5-23.

5. Choose File⇨Export⇨Change File Type⇨Template.

6. Click the Save As button.

The Save As dialog box opens, with the appropriate file type already selected.

7. Navigate to the location where you store your personal templates.

See Step 2 in the previous exercise for assistance in determining that location if needed.

Figure 5-21

8. **In the File Name box, type** Chapter 5 Blue **and then click Save.**

    The new template is saved.

9. **Choose File⇨Close to close the template.**

10. **Choose File⇨New and then click the Personal heading.**

    Your new template appears as a thumbnail image.

11. **Click the Chapter 5 Blue template to create a new document based upon it.**

12. **Close the new document without saving.**

Exit Word.

Figure 5-22

Figure 5-23

Summing Up

Styles and templates are two time-saving features in Word that help you easily and quickly apply consistent formatting and other settings. Here are the key points from this chapter:

- ✔ You can apply styles from the Styles gallery on the Home tab or from the Styles pane.

- ✔ To modify a style, select it in the Styles pane, and then open its shortcut menu (right-click or use the arrow) and choose Modify.

- ✔ To create a new style, use the New Style button at the bottom of the Styles pane.

- ✔ You can define a new style by example or by manually specifying a style definition.

- ✔ To import styles from other documents, click the Manage Styles button at the bottom of the Styles pane and then click Import/Export.

- ✔ Use the Style Inspector to check a paragraph's formatting. Click the Style Inspector button at the bottom of the Styles pane to open it.

- ✔ To modify an existing template, open it in Word and make changes. Make sure you open it as a template rather than just starting a new document based upon it.

- ✔ To create a new template, format a document the way you want it and then click Save As to save it as a template.

Try-it-yourself lab

For more practice with the features covered in this chapter, try the following exercise on your own:

1. **Research a new technology or medical advance on the Internet that interests you.**

2. **Using Word, write a report that summarizes what you learned. Use Word's built-in styles to format the report (Title, Heading 1, Heading 2, and so on).**

 If you don't want to spend a lot of time writing a report, grab some text from any document or website you have handy, and copy and paste it into Word. For example, you might get some book text from Project Gutenberg (www.gutenberg.org).

3. Create a new style and name it *Body.* Format it using a different font than the Normal style uses and apply the Body style to all the body paragraphs in your document.

4. Center the document title at the top of the document.

5. Write your name above the title, format it with the Subtitle style, and right-align it. Then redefine the Subtitle style to include the right-alignment.

6. Save your document as Chapter 5 Lab Report.

7. Delete all the text from the document and save the empty document (containing the different style definitions) as a template dubbed Lab Reports.

8. Close Word, saving all changes if prompted.

Know this tech talk

character style: A style that contains only text-level formatting.

paragraph style: A style that contains paragraph-level formatting; it may or may not also contain text-level formatting.

style: A named set of formatting specifications stored with a template or document.

Style gallery: A short list of commonly used styles appearing on the Home tab.

Style Inspector: A floating pane you can enable that shows what paragraph-level and text-level formatting is applied to the selected text.

template: A reusable model on which to create documents, containing styles, initial settings like margin and paper size, and in some cases sample text.

Chapter 6

Shaping Pages and Sections

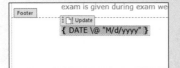

↙ Adding a page border or background *makes a text-heavy page look more attractive and graphical.*

↙ Headers and footers enable you to *place repeated information at the top or bottom of each page, respectively.*

↙ Inserting section breaks in a document enables you to *use different page settings for different parts* of the same document.

↙ Formatting text in multiple columns allows you to *create interesting and complex newsletter-type layouts.*

Your documents might require special pages or sections in any number of scenarios. Here are just a few examples: a distinctive page border that sets off a special section, a report with a cover page and a header, and a flyer that switches from one to two columns on a single page.

This chapter explains how you set up these pages and sections. After you understand how the page and section features work, you gain flexibility over the look and feel of your documents.

TIP

If you're preparing a lengthy report, check out Chapter 10, too. There, you find details about how to create a table of contents and an index, and how to organize figures and footnotes.

Formatting Pages

Each document has some basic properties that describe its pages, such as paper size, page orientation, and margins. You learn about these in Chapter 2. In this chapter, you look at a few of the less common page formatting settings: borders, backgrounds, and vertical alignment.

REMEMBER

Page settings are usually document-wide, but you can use sections (which I cover later in this chapter) to enable you to have different page border, page background, and/or vertical alignment settings within the same document.

Adding a page border

Page borders are primarily for decoration; you can use any style, color, and line thickness you want. You can also apply graphical borders (or border art) that repeat a small image as a pattern.

LINGO

A **page border** is a border that appears outside the margins on each page. **Border art** is a repeated small image that forms a border around the outside of the document margins.

The border art supplied with Word includes a variety of small graphics that look good when repeated around the edges of the page. One nice thing about using these, as opposed to manually placing images around the border, is that you can resize the entire border at once by changing the value in the Width box.

In the following exercise, you create several types of page borders.

Files needed: None

1. **Start Word, if necessary, and start a new blank document. Save the document as Chapter 6 Pages.**

2. **Choose Design⇨Page Borders.**

   The Borders and Shading dialog box opens with the Page Border tab selected.

3. **In the Style section, scroll down and select the double wavy line. Then from the Color drop-down list, choose Blue, Accent 5.**

4. **If a preview of a blue wavy line doesn't appear in the Preview area, click the Box button to apply the current settings to all sides of the page (see Figure 6-1).**

EXTRA INFO

Some line styles have a variety of widths you can choose from; the double wavy line you select in Step 3 has only one width available.

Figure 6-1

PRACTICE

For extra practice, try clicking the None icon and then clicking one or more individual sides in the Preview area. This is how you apply a page border to only certain sides of the page. When you're done experimenting with that, click the Box icon again to apply the border to all sides again.

5. Click OK.

The border is applied to the blank page. See Figure 6-2. Zoom in to see it better if desired.

Zoom in to see page
border more clearly.

Figure 6-2

Page borders, like many page-level formatting elements, appear only in certain views. You don't see them in Draft, Web Layout, or Outline view.

6. Choose Design➪Page Borders to reopen the Borders and Shading dialog box.

7. From the Art drop-down list, choose the palm trees; click the down increment arrow on the Width box to set the width to 28 points; and then click OK.

The palm tree border is applied to the page, as shown in Figure 6-3.

Figure 6-3

Leave the document open for the next exercise.

Applying a page background

Page backgrounds enable you to apply a color fill to the background of each page. This color fill can be a solid color, a gradient, a pattern, a texture, or even a picture. This background doesn't print by default, but you can change Word's settings to make the background print if you want. In Word 2013, the page background is referred to as the page color.

LINGO

A **page background,** or **page color,** is a fill to the background of a page.

Printing the background may use a lot of ink in your printer. This can get expensive, especially if you use an inkjet printer.

In the following exercise, you apply a page background and set up Word to print it.

Files needed: Chapter 6 Pages.docx, open from the preceding exercise

1. **In the Chapter 6 Pages document, choose Design⇨Page Color.**

   A palette of colors appears; see Figure 6-4.

2. **Click any color you like.**

   The page background changes to that color.

3. **Choose Design⇨Page Color⇨More Colors.**

   The Colors dialog box opens.

4. **Click the Custom tab; enter the following values: Red 230, Green 230, Blue 100 (see Figure 6-5); and then click OK.**

   The background changes to a shade of yellow.

5. **Choose Design⇨Page Color⇨Fill Effects.**

   The Fill Effects dialog box opens.

6. **Click the Texture tab, click the Newsprint texture (see Figure 6-6), and then click OK.**

   The background changes to the Newsprint texture.

TIP

If you have your own texture files, you can use them. Click the Other Texture button to browse for the files on your hard drive.

7. **Choose Design⇨Page Color⇨Fill Effects.**

   The Fill Effects dialog box opens.

8. **Click the Gradient tab and then select the Preset option.**

Figure 6-4

Figure 6-5

9. **From the Preset Colors drop-down list, choose Calm Water; in the Shading Styles area, select Diagonal Up (see Figure 6-7); and then click OK to apply the gradient background to the document.**

You can also define your own gradients by selecting One Color or Two Colors and then picking the colors to use. For more practice, try creating a gradient out of two of your favorite colors.

10. **Choose File⇨Print.**

Notice that the print preview doesn't include the background.

11. **Click Options to display the Word Options dialog box.**

12. **Click Display in the navigation pane at the left.**

13. **Select the Print Background Colors and Images check box (see Figure 6-8) and then click OK.**

14. **Choose File⇨Print again.**

Notice that this time print preview does include the background.

Newsprint texture

Figure 6-6

Figure 6-7

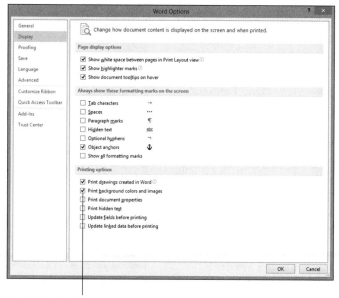

Mark this check box to print the page color.

Figure 6-8

15. **Click the Home tab to leave Backstage view without printing, repeat Steps 12 through 13, and deselect the Print Background Colors and Images check box.**

16. **Save the document and close it.**

Leave Word open for the next exercise.

Setting a page's vertical alignment

As you learn in Chapter 4, each paragraph has a horizontal alignment setting such as left-aligned, right-aligned, centered, or justified. This setting controls where the paragraph aligns in relation to the left and right margins.

Similarly, a document page has a vertical alignment that determines how the page's content aligns in relation to the top and bottom margins. The default setting is Top, which means the text begins at the top margin, but you can change that. For example, when typing a cover page or creating a flyer, you might want the text centered vertically.

LINGO

Vertical alignment is the way the page's content aligns with the top and bottom margins.

In the following exercise, you set the vertical alignment in a document.

Files needed: Chapter 6 Sign.docx

1. **Open the Chapter 6 Sign document and save it as Chapter 6 Door Sign.**

2. **Choose View⇨One Page so you can see the entire page at once.**

   Notice the text is top-aligned on the page.

3. **On the Page Layout tab, click the dialog box launcher in the Page Setup group.**

   The Page Setup dialog box opens.

4. **Click the Layout tab, choose Center from the Vertical Alignment drop-down list (see Figure 6-9), and then click OK.**

   The text is centered vertically on the page.

5. **Save the document and close it.**

Leave Word open for the next exercise.

Figure 6-9

Designing Headers and Footers

The header is the area at the top of a page, and the footer is the area at the bottom, outside of the top and bottom margins. Every document has a header and footer area, which are both empty by default.

The header and footer appear in Print Layout and Web Layout views, in Read Mode, and also on the printed page. (If you're in Draft view, you might want to switch to Print Layout view to follow along in this section more easily.)

LINGO

Headers and **footers** contain content that repeats at the top and bottom of each page, respectively, outside of the top and bottom margins.

You can place text in the header and footer that repeats on every page (or just certain pages), and you can insert a variety of codes in them that display information like page numbers, dates, and times. Watermarks are also part of a header, even though watermarks typically extend outside the header area.

Numbering the pages

Have you ever dropped a stack of papers that needed to stay in a certain order? If the pages were numbered, putting them back together was fairly simple. If not, what a frustrating, time-consuming task.

Fortunately, Word makes it very easy to number your document pages. And you can choose from a variety of numbering styles and formats. When you number pages in Word, you don't have to manually type the numbers onto each page. Instead, you place a code in the document that numbers the pages automatically. Sweet!

When you use the Page Numbering feature in Word, it automatically inserts the proper code in either the header or the footer so that each page is numbered consecutively.

Page numbers are visible only in Print Layout view, Read Mode, Print Preview, and on the printouts themselves. You don't see the page numbers if you're working in Draft view or Web Layout view, even though they're still present in the document.

In the following exercise, you place a page numbering code in a document's footer.

Files needed: Chapter 6 Syllabus.docx

1. **Open the Chapter 6 Syllabus document and save it as Chapter 6 Syllabus Pages.**

2. **Choose Insert⇨Page Number⇨Bottom of Page⇨Plain Number 3 (see Figure 6-10).**

   A page number code is placed at the right side of the footer, and the footer becomes active. Zoom in if needed to get a better look at it. See Figure 6-11.

You can't edit the body of the document while you're in this mode. To resume working within the main part of the document, double-click the main document (anywhere below the header or above the footer).

The page number code is gray when you select it; that's your clue that it's a code and not regular text.

Figure 6-10

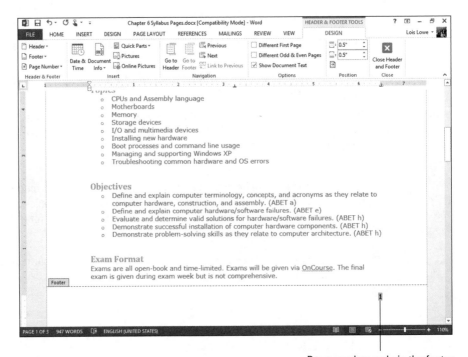

Page number code in the footer

Figure 6-11

3. Double-click anywhere in the main part of the document to leave the footer.

The body of the document becomes editable again, and the actual page numbers appear at the bottoms of the pages.

For more practice, choose Insert⇨Page Number⇨Remove Page Numbers to undo the page number insertion and then choose a different preset from the Bottom of Page submenu. Not all the presets are plain; some of them add formatting.

Leave the document open for the next exercise.

In Figure 6-10, notice the other page number position options instead of Bottom of Page:

- ✔ **Top of Page:** Places the page number code in the *header* (at the top of the page). The page numbers appear on every page.

- ✔ **Page Margins:** Places the page number code on the side of the page. The page numbers appear on every page.

- ✔ **Current Position:** Places the page number code at the insertion point in the document (as a one-time thing). Because the code is not in the header or footer, it doesn't repeat on each page. You might use this to create a cross-reference to content that's on another page, for example.

- ✔ **Format Page Numbers:** Opens a dialog box where you can fine-tune the formatting of the page numbering code, such as using Roman numerals or letters instead of digits.

- ✔ **Remove Page Numbers:** Removes existing page numbering code(s).

Selecting a header or footer preset

In addition to a page number, you can put other content in the header and footer areas of your document. For example, if you're typing the minutes of a club meeting, you might want to put the club's name in the header so that it appears across the top of each page.

Here are two ways of putting content into the header or footer:

- ✔ Choose presets to insert codes and formatting.

- ✔ Type text and insert codes manually into the headers and footers.

In the following exercise, you use a header preset.

Files needed: Chapter 6 Syllabus Pages.docx, open from the preceding exercise

1. **In the Chapter 6 Syllabus Pages document, choose Insert⇨Header⇨ Banded.**

   Placeholder text and a colored bar appear in the Header section, and the Header section becomes active. See Figure 6-12.

Figure 6-12

Some of the presets for headers and footers also insert a page-numbering code. This saves you the step of inserting the page-numbering code separately.

2. **Click in the *[DOCUMENT TITLE]* placeholder and then type** CIT 233 SYLLABUS.

3. **Choose Header & Footer Tools Design⇨Close Header and Footer.**

   This is an alternative way to return to normal editing mode.

Leave the document open for the next exercise.

Creating a custom header or footer

The header and footer presets are great if they happen to match what you want to place there, but you can also create your own custom headers and footers that contain the exact combination of text and codes that you need. To do so, open the header or footer, click in it, and then type the text you want. Use the buttons on the Header & Footer Tools Design tab to insert codes.

In the following exercise, you create a custom footer that uses a combination of date/time codes, page numbers, and typed text.

Files needed: Chapter 6 Syllabus Pages.docx, open from the preceding exercise

1. **In the Chapter 6 Syllabus Pages document, double-click at the bottom of the first page to open the footer and move the insertion point into it.**

2. **Select the page number that's already there and press the Delete key.**

3. **Press the Backspace key twice to move the insertion point to the left side of the footer.**

4. **Choose Header & Footer Tools Design⇨Date & Time.**

Figure 6-13

   The Date and Time dialog box opens (see Figure 6-13).

5. **Make sure that the Update Automatically check box is selected, click the first date format on the list, and then click OK.**

   A code for the date appears in the footer.

TIP

You can tell it's a code rather than plain text because when you point to it, it appears with a gray background.

6. **Right-click the date code and choose Toggle Field Codes.**

   This lets you see the code that creates the date. See Figure 6-14.

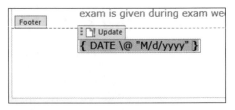

7. **Click in the date code and click the Update text that appears above it.**

Figure 6-14

   The date code is updated and returns to showing the date itself rather than the code.

8. **Click to the right of the date code to move the insertion point there and then press the Tab key to move to the center of the footer.**

9. **Type** Lawrence College **and press Tab to move to the right of the footer.**

The headers and footers have preset tab stops — a center-aligned one in the center, and a right-aligned one at the right. When you press Tab in Steps 8 and 9, you're moving to those existing tab stops.

10. **Choose Header & Footer Tools Design⇨Page Number⇨Current Position⇨Plain Number.**

   A page number code is inserted.

If you're curious about the code behind the page number, right-click it and choose Toggle Field Codes, as you did with the date in Step 6. Click the Toggle Field Codes button again to return to normal viewing.

11. **Choose Header & Footer Tools Design⇨Close Header and Footer and then choose File⇨Print and check the preview at the right.**

   Notice that the codes in the footer produce today's date and the current page number on each page.

12. **Click the Back button or press Esc to leave Backstage view without printing.**

Leave the document open for the next exercise.

In a complex document, you can get very fancy with headers and footers. For example, you can choose to have a different header and footer on the first page, and you can have different headers and footers on odd and even pages. That's handy when you're printing a double-sided booklet, for example, so the page numbers can always be on the outside edges. To set either of those options, select their check boxes on the Header & Footer Tools Design tab. See Figure 6-15.

Figure 6-15

You can also create section breaks, and have a different header and footer in each section. (I cover sections later in this chapter.) When you use multiple headers and footers in a document, you can move among them by clicking the Previous and Next buttons on the Header & Footer Tools Design tab.

To adjust the header and footer size and positioning, use the settings in the Position group on the Header & Footer Tools Design tab. Refer to Figure 6-15. You can specify a Header from Top and Footer from Bottom position there. For example, if you want a taller header section, increase the Header from Top setting.

Inserting a watermark

Watermarks, which display a faint picture or text phrase behind the regular text, are used for a variety of purposes in documents. Some high-end paper has an embossed logo on it, and a watermark created via computer can approximate that look. Watermarks are also used to mark documents with designations, such as DRAFT or CONFIDENTIAL.

> **LINGO**
>
> A **watermark** is a faint image that appears behind the regular text on the page.

Watermarks are stored in a document's header/footer, so you can edit a watermark, including adjusting its position, when in Header and Footer editing mode.

In the following exercise, you place a watermark on a document.

Files needed: Chapter 6 Syllabus Pages.docx, open from the preceding exercise

1. **In the Chapter 6 Syllabus Pages document, choose Design⇨ Watermark⇨Draft 1.**

   See Figure 6-16. You might need to scroll down on the list to find Draft 1. The word DRAFT appears in gray behind the text on each page.

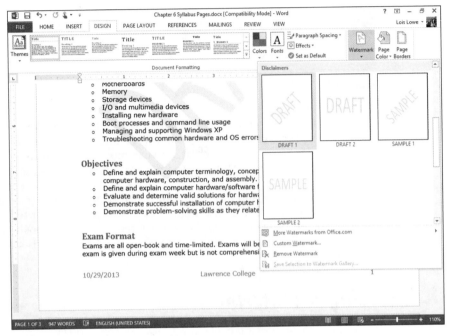

Figure 6-16

2. **Choose Design⇨Watermark⇨Remove Watermark.**

3. **Choose Design⇨Watermark⇨Custom Watermark.**

    The Printed Watermark dialog box opens.

4. **Select the Text Watermark option; in the Text box, delete the existing text and type** Lawrence College **(see Figure 6-17); and then click OK.**

    The watermark is inserted.

5. **Double-click the document's header area to enter Header and Footer editing mode and then click the watermark twice to select it.**

    Notice that selection handles appear around the watermark.

Figure 6-17

A watermark is really just a piece of WordArt; you can edit its text —
including rotating it, changing its color, and so on — as you would any
WordArt. Notice that the WordArt Tools Format tab becomes available
when you select the watermark.

6. **Choose WordArt Tools Format⇨WordArt Shape Fill and then click the Red, Accent 2, Lighter 80% color (see Figure 6-18).**

Red, Accent 2, Lighter 80%

Figure 6-18

PRACTICE

For more practice, try some of the other WordArt formatting options on
the watermark, such as WordArt Styles or Change Shape.

7. **Choose Header & Footer Tools Design⇨Close Header and Footer to return to normal editing.**

8. **Save the document and close it.**

Leave Word open for the next exercise.

Working with Multisection Documents

You can set many page layout properties, such as margins, number of columns, headers and footers, paper size, and page orientation, for the entire document. However, in some situations, you might like to have different page layout settings within the same document, such as with a letter and envelope stored together in one file.

When you need to have different page layout settings in the same document, you can create a section break. A section break enables you to define different settings for different areas of a document.

LINGO

A **section break** is a nonprinting marker in a document that indicates where new settings, such as different margins, page orientation, or column numbers, should take effect.

Viewing section breaks and other hidden characters

Word automatically creates section breaks when you use certain features, so you may have created section breaks in the past and not realized it. For example, when you add an envelope to the document, which I cover in Chapter 9, a section break is automatically inserted to separate the envelope from the letter. When you select some paragraphs and choose a different number of columns for them, as you learn later in this chapter, section breaks are created before and after the selected paragraphs, and the new number-of-columns setting is applied to only the midsection between the two section breaks. Within Word, many features create section breaks for you.

In the following exercise, you view a section break and turn on the display of other hidden characters.

Files needed: Chapter 6 Envelope.docx

1. **Open the Chapter 6 Envelope document and then choose View➪Draft to switch to Draft view.**

   A section break line becomes visible between the envelope text and the letter text.

2. **On the Home tab, click the Show/Hide button.**

   Hidden characters, such as paragraph breaks and line breaks, appear. See Figure 6-19.

Show/Hide button

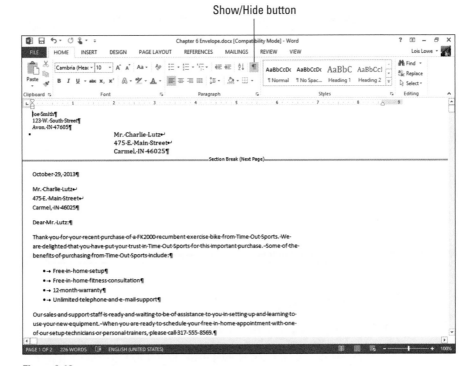

Figure 6-19

3. **Click the Show/Hide button again to toggle off the hidden characters and then choose View⇨Print Layout to switch back to Print Layout view.**

4. **Close the document. Do not save changes if prompted.**

Leave Word open for the next exercise.

Inserting a section break

Word enables you to create several types of section breaks. Table 6-1 explains what your options are, what they do, and when you might use each type of break.

Table 6-1	Types of Section Breaks	
Type	*What This Section Break Does*	*Example*
Next page	Starts the section on a new page.	Separate the envelope from the letter in the preceding exercise.
Continuous	Creates a section break that does not start a new page.	Separate a one-column masthead on a newsletter from a three-column news story beneath it.
Even page	Starts the new section on an even-numbered page.	If the current page is odd-numbered, it's the same as a regular Next-page break. If the current page is even-numbered, it results in two page breaks.
Odd page	Starts the new section on an odd-numbered page.	Most books begin a new chapter on an odd-numbered page.

In this exercise, you create a Next page section break.

Files needed: Chapter 6 Newsletter.docx

1. **Open the Chapter 6 Newsletter document and save it as Chapter 6 Newsletter Breaks.**

2. **Scroll down to the Ink heading on page 4, place the insertion point immediately before it, and choose Page Layout⇨Breaks⇨Next Page.**

   A section break is inserted that starts the next section on a new page.

   Note: If the hidden characters are still displaying from the previous exercise, click the Show/Hide button on the Home tab or press Ctrl+Shift+8 to turn them off.

3. **Choose View⇨Draft to switch to Draft view so you can see the break (see Figure 6-20).**

4. **Click the break to select it and then press the Delete key.**

   The break is removed.

Leave the document open for the next exercise.

Section break

Figure 6-20

Formatting Text in Multiple Columns

One of the benefits of a section break is that it lets you set certain areas of a document in different columns than the rest. You can create the section break first and then change the number of columns in that section; or you can select the text that should be differently columned and then change the column setting, and Word will create the section breaks as needed.

In this exercise, you change the Columns setting for part of a document.

Files needed: Chapter 6 Newsletter Breaks.docx, open from the preceding exercise

1. **In the Chapter 6 Newsletter Breaks document, choose View⇨Draft to switch to Draft view, if you're not already in Draft view.**

2. **Scroll to the top of the first page and place the insertion point at the beginning of the *Bring your best ideas to life* heading line.**

3. **Choose Page Layout⇨Breaks⇨Continuous.**

   A continuous section break is inserted. Because you're in Draft view, you can see it; you couldn't see it in Print Layout view.

To check, switch to Print Layout view and then switch back to Draft view.

4. **Choose Page Layout⇨Columns⇨Two.**

   The text in the section that follows the section break changes to a two-column layout, and the view switches automatically to Print Layout, as shown in Figure 6-21.

Figure 6-21

For more practice, try each of the other settings on the Columns menu. Return to the Two setting when finished experimenting.

5. **Select the heading, THE MICROSOFT OFFICE BACKSTAGE VIEW, on page 4, and everything below it to the next heading.**

   Select up to, but not including, the Recover unsaved work heading.

6. **Choose Page Layout⇨Columns One.**

   The selected text changes to a single-column layout; the rest of the document stays the same.

7. **Choose View⇨Draft and notice the section breaks that Word automatically inserted.**

   Continuous section breaks appear at the beginning and end of the selected text.

8. **Choose View⇨Print Layout to return to Print Layout view.**

9. **Save the document and close it.**

Exit Word.

 # *Summing Up*

Word's Page Layout features enable you to set up each page with the exact borders, margins, columns, headers, and footers you want. Here's a summary of what you learn in this chapter:

- ✔ To create a page border, choose Design⇨Page Borders. You can either use a regular line as a border (with any color, thickness, and style you want), or choose one of the border art images Word provides.

- ✔ To apply a page background, choose Design⇨Page Color. You can use a plain color, a pattern, a gradient, a texture, or a picture.

- ✔ To set the vertical alignment for the page layout, click the dialog box launcher in the Page Setup group on the Page Layout tab, and then on the Layout tab, set the Vertical Alignment setting.

- ✔ Choose Insert⇨Header or Insert⇨Footer to use preset headers and footers, respectively.

- ✔ Choose Insert⇨Page Number to place page numbering codes in the header or footer.

- ✔ To edit a header or footer manually, in Print Layout view, double-click the header or footer area to open it for editing.

- ✔ A watermark is a faint image that appears behind the regular text. Choose Design⇨Watermark to insert one.

✔ Watermarks are stored in the header/footer of the document, so while the header and footer are active, you can also edit the watermark.

✔ You can insert section breaks by choosing Page Layout⇨Breaks. You can then apply different page layout formatting to each section.

✔ Section breaks are also automatically created when you select text and then change the number of columns for that text (choose Page Layout⇨Columns).

Try-it-yourself lab

For more practice with the features covered in this chapter, try the following exercise on your own:

1. **Start Word and type the title of a newsletter that you want to create.**

   The newsletter can be on any subject of interest to you. Make the title big and bold, so it stretches all the way across the page.

2. **Below the title, type a newsletter article.**

3. **Using section breaks and the Columns feature, format the article so that it appears in three columns under the newsletter title, while the title itself remains in one column.**

4. **Save your document as Chapter 6 Lab and close it.**

5. **Close all documents and exit Word.**

Know this tech talk

footer: The area below the bottom margin of a page, where repeated information can optionally be placed.

header: The area above the top margin of a page, where repeated information can optionally be placed.

page border: A border that appears outside the margins on each page of the document.

section break: A marker in a document that divides the document into multiple sections. Each section can have its own page layout settings.

vertical alignment: The alignment of the page's content in relation to its top and bottom margins.

watermark: A faint image of text or a graphic that appears behind the text on a page.

Creating Tables

✔ Using tables allows you to *organize complex sets of data in an orderly fashion.*

✔ Inserting a table is an easy way to *create a standard table of any size.*

✔ Drawing a table enables you to *customize the row and column dividers.*

✔ You can resize rows and columns to *make a table's structure meet your needs.*

✔ Formatting table borders *allows you to emphasize or hide certain lines of the table.*

*W*ord can create tables with rows and columns, somewhat like a spreadsheet (although Word can't perform calculations or execute functions the way spreadsheets do). In Word, tables are useful for organizing information in multicolumn layouts, such as address lists and schedules. You may be surprised at all the uses you can find for tables in your documents!

In this chapter, you learn how to insert tables in several ways. You also learn how to modify a table, and how to apply formatting to it that makes it easier to read and understand.

Inserting or Drawing a Table

To create a table, you can either insert one as a whole or draw one line by line. In most cases, if you want a *standard-looking table* (that is, one with equally sized rows and columns), your best bet is to insert it. If you want an *unusual-looking table,* such as with different numbers of columns in some rows, you may be better off drawing the table.

When inserting a new table, you can specify a number of rows and columns to create a blank grid, and then fill in the grid by typing. Press the Tab key to move to the next cell. When you reach the end of the last row, you can press Tab to add a row to the table.

In the following exercise, you create a new table in two ways.

Files needed: None

1. **Start a new blank document in Word and save it as Chapter 7 Table.**

2. **Choose Insert⇨Table, and in the menu that appears with a grid, drag across the grid to select three rows and three columns, as shown in Figure 7-1, and then release the mouse button to create the table.**

Figure 7-1

PRACTICE

For extra practice, delete the table you just inserted (press Ctrl+Z to undo the last action) and then insert the table by choosing Insert➪Table➪Insert Table. A dialog box where you can enter the number of rows and columns as digits opens.

3. **In the first cell of the first row, type** Name **and then press the Tab key to move to the next column.**

4. **Type** Position, **press Tab, type** Active?, **and press Tab.**

The insertion point moves to the first cell in the next row.

5. **Type the rest of the entries shown in Figure 7-2 into the table. When you reach the bottom-right cell, press Tab again to create the extra row needed.**

A new row appears at the bottom of the table.

Name	Position	Active?
Sheldon Peterson	Catcher	Yes
Brendon Lowe	Pitcher	Yes
Peter Fitzgerald	First Base	Yes
John Wilson	Second Base	No

Figure 7-2

6. **Click below the table to move the insertion point and then choose Insert➪Table➪Draw Table.**

The mouse pointer turns into a pencil symbol.

7. **Drag to draw a box that's approximately the same height and width as the table you created earlier.**

A box appears, and the mouse pointer remains a pencil.

8. **Drag within the box to draw three vertical lines and two horizontal lines, as shown in Figure 7-3.**

Notice that the rightmost vertical line spans only the bottom two rows.

Figure 7-3

9. **Press Esc to turn off the drawing mode, and then type the text shown in Figure 7-4 into the new table.**

Shift	Location	Worker	
Day	Clermont	Tom	Jones
Day	Clermont	Alice	Little

Figure 7-4

10. **Save the changes to the document and close it.**

Leave Word open for the next exercise.

Converting Text to a Table

If you already have some text that's separated into rows and columns with tabs, commas, or some other consistent character, you can convert it to a table with a few simple clicks.

For conversion to work, the existing text must be *delimited* with a consistent character to separate the columns. For example, the text in Figure 7-5 shows the data from the first table in the preceding exercise as a delimited text file. The tab stops mark where each column should break, so that the data is organized into three columns. The hidden tab and paragraph markers are displayed to make the tab characters more obvious here.

LINGO

Delimited means separated via a consistent scheme.

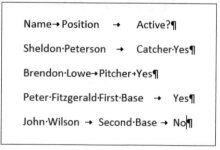

Name→Position → Active?¶

Sheldon·Peterson → Catcher·Yes¶

Brendon·Lowe→Pitcher→Yes¶

Peter·Fitzgerald·First·Base → Yes¶

John·Wilson → Second·Base → No¶

Figure 7-5

In the following exercise, you convert some existing delimited text into a table.

Files needed: Chapter 7 Schedule.docx.

1. **Open Chapter 7 Schedule and save it as Chapter 7 Schedule Table.**

2. **Select all the text in the document and then choose Insert⟹Table⟹ Convert Text to Table.**

The Convert Text to Table dialog box opens. See Figure 7-6.

3. Click OK.

The text converts to a five-column table.

4. Save the changes to the document.

Leave the document open for the next exercise.

If you don't get the results you expect when converting text to a table, your rows probably contain an inconsistent number of delimiters. You may be missing a tab or have two tabs in a row, for example. Press Ctrl+Z to undo the table creation, check your column markers, and try again. You can turn on the display of hidden characters from the Home tab's Show/Hide button. Doing so helps you see where the tabs are.

Figure 7-6

Selecting Rows and Columns

Working with a table often involves selecting one or more cells, rows, or columns. Here are the many ways to do this:

- ✔ Drag across the cells you want to select.

- ✔ Click in the upper-left cell you want to select, press the Shift key, and then press arrow keys to extend the selection.

- ✔ Click outside of the table on the left side to select an entire row.

- ✔ Click outside of the table above the table to select an entire column.

- ✔ Click the table selector (the four-headed arrow in a box; see Figure 7-7) in the upper-left corner of the table to select the entire table.

Table selector

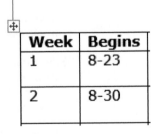

Week	Begins
1	8-23
2	8-30

Figure 7-7

In the following exercise, you practice selecting various parts of a table.

Files needed: Chapter 7 Schedule Table.docx, open from the preceding exercise

1. **In Chapter 7 Schedule Table, click inside any cell of the table and then click the table selector icon (refer to Figure 7-7).**

   The entire table is selected.

2. **Click away from the table to deselect it.**

3. **Position the mouse pointer to the left of the table, next to the third row (Week 2), and click.**

   That row becomes selected. See Figure 7-8.

   New in Word 2013, when you select a row as in Figure 7-8, an Add Row indicator appears (the plus sign inside a circle on the left edge of the table). You could click that symbol to insert a new row, although that's not what you're doing in this exercise.

Week	Begins	Read	Do Labs	What's Due
1	8-23	Chapters 1 and 2	1.1, 1.3, 1.4, 2.1, 2.2, 2.3, 2.4	Introduce yourself to your classmates in the Forum area
2	8-30	Chapter 4	4.1, 4.3, 4.4, 4.5	
3	9-6	Chapter 5	5.1, 5.2, 5.6	

Figure 7-8

4. **Drag the mouse downward to row 5 (Week 4).**

   Rows 4 and 5 also become selected.

5. **Position the mouse pointer above the first column so the pointer becomes a black down-pointing arrow, and click.**

   The first column becomes selected.

6. **Click in the first cell and press the Shift key. Press the left-arrow key twice to extend the selection and then press the down-arrow key once to extend the selection.**

7. **Click in the first cell again and drag down to the third cell in the third row to extend the selection.**

8. **Click in any unselected cell to cancel the previous selections.**

Leave the document open for the next exercise.

Resizing Rows and Columns

Word handles row height automatically for you, so you usually don't have to think about it. The row height changes as needed to accommodate the font size of the text in the cells of that row. Text in a cell wraps automatically to the next line when it runs out of room horizontally, so you can expect your table rows to expand in height as you type more text into them.

WARNING!

If you manually resize a row's height, the ability to auto-resize to fit content is turned off for that row. Therefore, if you add more text to that row later, Word doesn't automatically expand that row's height to accommodate it, and some text may be truncated.

In contrast, column width remains fixed until you change it, regardless of the cell's content. If you want the width of a column to change, you must change it yourself.

In the following exercise, you resize the rows and columns of a table.

Files needed: Chapter 7 Schedule Table.docx, open from the preceding exercise

1. **In Chapter 7 Schedule Table, position the mouse pointer over the column divider between the first and second columns.**

   The mouse pointer becomes a double-headed arrow, as shown in Figure 7-9.

2. **Drag to the right slightly to increase the width of the first column by about ¼ inch.**

   Notice that the second column's heading in the first row now wraps unattractively, as shown in Figure 7-10.

3. **Press Ctrl+Z to undo the column width change. While pressing the Shift key, repeat Steps 1 and 2.**

   The other columns shift to the right to make room for the new width because the Shift key is pressed.

4. **Select the cells containing 1 and 2 in the first column.**

5. **Drag the column divider between the first and second columns to the left about ¼ inch, dragging that column back to its original position.**

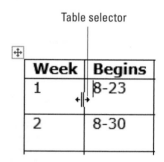

Table selector

Week	Begins
1	8-23
2	8-30

Figure 7-9

Table selector

Week	Begins
1	8-23
2	8-30

Figure 7-10

Only the two rows where cells were selected are affected, as shown in Figure 7-11.

6. **Press Ctrl+Z to undo the column change; click to move the insertion point inside any cell in the first column.**

7. **Choose Table Tools Layout⇨AutoFit⇨ AutoFit Contents, as shown in Figure 7-12.**

All the column widths are adjusted in the table to fit the content more compactly.

8. **Press Ctrl+Z to undo the resizing; double-click the column divider between the first and second columns.**

This time only column 1 resizes to fit its contents more compactly.

Only the selected
rows are adjusted.

Figure 7-11

Figure 7-12

9. **Position the mouse pointer over the horizontal divider between the heading row at the top and the first data row.**

The mouse pointer becomes a two-headed arrow (see Figure 7-13).

10. **Drag downward to increase the height of the heading row by about ¼ inch.**

11. **Select the heading row, and choose Table Tools Layout⇨Align Bottom Left.**

The headings are bottom-aligned in their cells (see Figure 7-14). Vertical alignment was not an issue previously because the height of the row was auto-fitted to the content.

Mouse pointer

Week	Begins
1	8-23
2	8-30

Figure 7-13

Align Bottom Left button

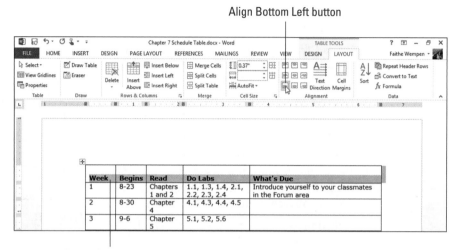

Text in first row is bottom-aligned vertically and left-aligned horizontally.

Figure 7-14

12. **Click the table selector icon in the upper-left corner of the table to select the entire table.**

13. **Choose Table Tools Layout⇨Distribute Columns to evenly distribute the space among all the columns (see Figure 7-15).**

Columns are now
all the same width.

Distribute Columns button

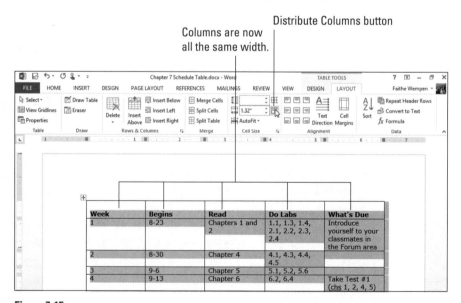

Figure 7-15

14. **Press Ctrl+Z to undo the distribute operation.**

15. **Save the changes to the document.**

Leave the document open for the next exercise.

Formatting Table Borders

Gridlines can be displayed or hidden onscreen (via Table Tools Layout⇨View Gridlines). Gridlines do not print, and when displayed onscreen, they appear as thin blue or gray dashed lines. You probably won't see the gridlines in most tables because they're covered by borders. By default, table gridlines have plain black borders. You can change the borders to different colors, styles (such as dotted or dashed), and thicknesses, or remove the borders altogether.

LINGO

Gridlines are the dividers that separate a table's rows and columns. A **border** is formatting applied to a gridline that makes it appear when printed.

In the following exercise, you apply formatting to table borders.

Files needed: Chapter 7 Schedule Table.docx, open from the preceding exercise

1. **In Chapter 7 Schedule Table, select the entire table and then choose Table Tools Design⇨Borders⇨No Border (see Figure 7-16).**

2. **If the gridlines aren't already visible, choose Table Tools Layout⇨View Gridlines.**

   Dashed lines appear for the table's row and column dividers. See Figure 7-17.

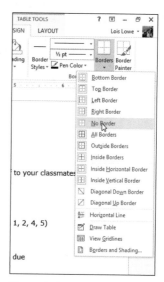

Figure 7-16

View Gridlines button

Gridlines appear.

Figure 7-17

3. **Select the header row of the table and then choose Table Tools Design⇨Line Weight⇨2¼ Pt (see Figure 7-18).**

4. **Choose Table Tools Design⇨Pen Color and click the red square in the Standard Colors section.**

5. **Choose Table Tools Design⇨Borders⇨ Bottom Border.**

   A red bottom border with 2¼-inch thickness appears on that row only.

6. **Select all the rows in the table *except* the header row, and then click the dialog box launcher for the Borders group on the Table Tools Design tab.**

   The Borders and Shading dialog box opens, with the Borders tab displayed. A red border appears in the sample for the top of the selection.

7. **From the Width drop-down list, choose ½ Pt.**

8. **In the Preview area, click the areas where vertical borders might appear (see Figure 7-19) and then click OK.**

Line Weight drop-down menu

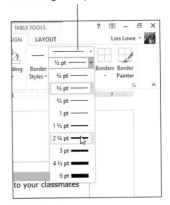

Figure 7-18

Click these three areas to
place vertical borders.

Figure 7-19

9. **Turn off the gridlines again by choosing Table Tools Layout⇨View Gridlines, and then click away from the table to deselect it.**

The table now has a thick, top border separating the header from the rest of the table, and red vertical lines separating the columns. See Figure 7-20.

Week	Begins	Read	Do Labs	What's Due
1	8-23	Chapters 1 and 2	1.1, 1.3, 1.4, 2.1, 2.2, 2.3, 2.4	Introduce yourself to your classmates in the Forum area
2	8-30	Chapter 4	4.1, 4.3, 4.4, 4.5	
3	9-6	Chapter 5	5.1, 5.2, 5.6	
4	9-13	Chapter 6	6.2, 6.4	Take Test #1 (chs 1, 2, 4, 5)
5	9-20	Assembly Language	Assembly project	
6	9-27	Chapter 7	7.1, 7.2, 7.5	Assembly projects due
7	10-4	Chapter 8	8.1, 8.2, 8.4, 8.6	
8	10-11	Chapter 9	9.1, 9.2, 9.3,	

Figure 7-20

10. **Save the changes to the document.**

Exit Word.

Summing Up

Tables can be a great way to organize data into multiple rows and columns. Here are the key points from this chapter:

- ✔ You can create a new table from the Insert tab, either by specifying a number of rows and columns, or by drawing the table.
- ✔ You can also convert existing delimited text into a table with the Convert Text to Table command.
- ✔ Drag the borders of a table to resize rows and columns.
- ✔ Tables have *gridlines* (or nonprinting lines that show where the rows and columns are) and, optionally, *borders* (formatting applied to the gridlines).
- ✔ Format a table's borders from the Table Tools Design tab.

Try-it-yourself lab

For more practice with the features covered in this chapter, try the following exercise on your own:

1. **In a new document, create a table with two columns and ten rows.**
2. **In the left column, type a list of items you want to purchase for your home.**
3. **In the right column, type the approximate price for each item.**
4. **Add a new row at the top of the table, and in the new row, type the columns' headings.**
5. **Format the table attractively.**
6. **Save your document with a name of your choice and then close Word.**

Know this tech talk

border: Formatting applied to the outer edge or gridline of a table cell or other object.

delimited: Multicolumn data where the columns are separated using a consistent character, such as a tab.

gridlines: The nonprinting lines that (optionally) appear onscreen where the edges of a table's rows and columns are.

table selector: The small square in the upper-left corner of a table that, when clicked, selects the entire table.

Chapter 8
Pepping Up the Page with Graphics

✔ Find and insert clip art from Microsoft's online collection *to use professionally designed artwork* without paying royalties or usage fees.

✔ Insert your own photos and other artwork in a Word document to *personalize your work and make it more interesting to view.*

✔ Change the text wrap settings for graphics to *fine-tune the way that the text in the document wraps* around and interacts with the graphics.

✔ Drawing lines and shapes with Word's Shapes tool *creates custom artwork* that you may not otherwise be able to find, such as unique logos.

✔ Apply fill colors and effects to drawn shapes to *make the drawings stand out.*

You can dress up Word documents with a variety of graphics by either importing pictures from other sources or creating them yourself inside Word. Graphics can make a document more interesting and can explain visual concepts more easily than text alone. (You know the old saying . . . a picture is worth a thousand words.)

In this chapter, you learn how to insert clip art and photos from your own files and how to position and format pictures in a document. You also learn about the drawing tools, which are available not only in Word, but also in Excel and PowerPoint.

TIP

If you're creating a report with graphics that illustrate the content, you'll also be interested in Word's features for numbering and captioning figures. See Chapter 10, which focuses on creating professional reports, for details.

Inserting Pictures from the Web

In Word 2013, and also in some of the other Office apps too, you get free access to a large online library of clip art maintained by Microsoft at Office.com. Each of the main Office applications has an Online Pictures command that opens a dialog box where you can search this library and insert images from it into your documents. This image library contains not only clip art but also royalty-free stock photography.

Office.com is only one of the possible sources of online images you can explore. You can also retrieve files via a Bing Image Search on the web. Bing (www.bing.com) is a search engine sponsored by Microsoft, and the Bing Image Search feature in Office applications enables you to easily locate images from all over the Internet.

LINGO

Clip art is generic artwork. In the days before most businesses had computers, companies that needed stock artwork would buy large books of line drawings, and when they needed an image, they would clip it out of the book with scissors and glue it to a paste-up layout. That's where the name comes from. Today, clip art refers to line-based drawings such as the ones you can get from Office.com.

Understanding vector and raster graphics

There are two types of computer graphics: vector and raster. They're very different from one another, and each is best suited for a different purpose.

Clip art is a type of vector graphic. A *vector* graphic is created behind the scenes by using math formulas; if you've taken a geometry class where you plotted a function on graph paper, you get the idea. Computerized clip art builds images by layering and combining individual lines and shapes, each one constructed via a math formula. As a result, the clips can be resized without losing any quality because resizing simply changes the math formula. Clip art files are also very small compared with raster graphics. The main drawback of clip art is that the images don't look real — they look like drawings.

Photos from digital cameras are examples of *raster* graphics. A raster graphic is a densely packed collection of colored dots that together form an image. If you zoom in on a photo on a computer, you can see these dots individually. In a raster graphic, each dot is called a *pixel,* and its color is represented by a numeric code (usually 24 or 32 binary digits in length per pixel).

Finding and inserting pictures from the web

In the following exercise, you practice searching for online pictures by using both Office.com and a Bing image search and inserting them in a document.

Files needed: Chapter 8 Breton.docx

1. **Open Chapter 8 Breton.docx and save it as Chapter 8 Breton Art.docx.**

2. **Position the insertion point at the beginning of the first body paragraph ("This week . . .").**

TIP

The picture will be placed wherever the insertion point is. If the insertion point is in the middle of a paragraph, the picture will split the paragraph in two, possibly creating an awkward look that you didn't intend. For best results in most cases, position the insertion point on its own line, between two paragraphs, or at least at the beginning or end of a paragraph.

3. **Choose Insert➪Online Pictures.**

   The Insert Pictures dialog box opens.

4. **Click in the Office.com Clip Art search box, type** poinsettia, **and press Enter.**

   A selection of pictures that have *poinsettia* as a keyword appear in the task pane. See Figure 8-1.

Figure 8-1

5. **Scroll through the resulting clips.**

   Notice that the results are a mixture of line drawings and photographs.

6. **Click one of the clips and then click the Insert button to insert it.**

   The clip appears in the document, as shown in Figure 8-2. If your clip is larger than the one shown, resize it by dragging one of its corners. See "Resizing a Picture" later in this chapter for help if needed.

LINGO

Notice that the clip is placed in the document as an **inline image**. An inline image is treated like a really large character of text. The height of the image makes the first line of the paragraph extra tall, as you can see in Figure 8-2. Later in this chapter, you learn how to make text wrap more gracefully around a picture.

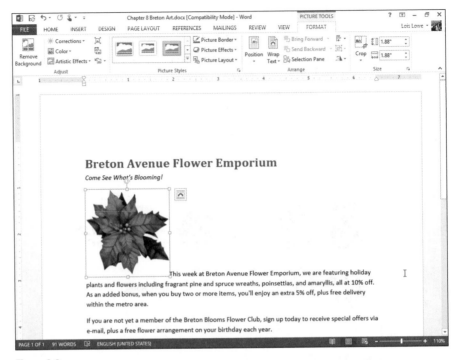

Figure 8-2

7. **Press Delete to remove the inserted clip.**

8. **Press Enter to create a new paragraph and then press the up-arrow key once to move the insertion point into that new paragraph.**

9. **Repeat Steps 2 through 5 to insert a different picture.**

   This time the clip appears on its own line.

10. **Press Delete to remove the inserted clip.**

11. **On the Insert tab, click Online Pictures.**

   The Insert Pictures dialog box opens.

12. **Click in the Bing Image Search box, type poinsettia, and press Enter.**

A selection of pictures that have *poinsettia* as a keyword appear in the task pane. See Figure 8-3.

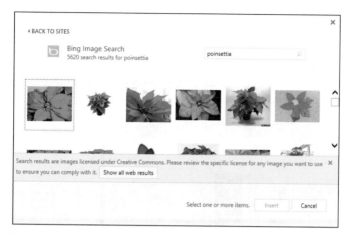

Figure 8-3

13. **Click one of the pictures and then click the Insert button to insert it.**

    The clip appears in the document. Depending on the picture you chose, the image may be small, as in Figure 8-2, or may take up the entire page width.

14. **Press Delete to remove the inserted clip and press Delete again to delete the blank line you created earlier.**

15. **Save the changes to the document.**

Leave the document open for the next exercise.

Inserting Photos from Files

The clips available online are generic. Sometimes, you might want to insert a more personal picture, such as a digital photo you took or a picture that a friend or coworker sent you via e-mail.

In the following exercise, you insert a photograph from a file stored on your hard drive.

Files needed: Chapter 8 Breton Art.docx, already open from the previous exercise

1. **In Chapter 8 Breton Art.docx, click at the end of the document and press Enter to start a new paragraph.**

2. **Choose Insert⇨Pictures.**

   The Insert Picture dialog box opens.

3. **Navigate to the folder containing the data files for this chapter and select 08graphic01.jpg, as shown in Figure 8-4.**

Figure 8-4

4. **Click the Insert button.**

   The picture is inserted in the document.

5. **Save the changes to the document.**

Leave the document open for the next exercise.

Managing Picture Size and Placement

After you insert a graphic in a document, you may decide you want to move it or change how the text around it interacts with it. For example, you might want the text to wrap around the graphic or even run on top of it.

You can size and position a graphic in several ways. You can manually size or move it by dragging; you can specify exact values for height, width, and/or position on the page; or you can use the Word placement commands to place the image in relation to other content.

Changing the text wrap setting for a picture

By default, as I mention earlier, a picture is inserted as an inline image, which means it's treated like a text character. However, that's not usually the best way for an image to interact with the text.

When you want the text to flow around an image, change the image's Text Wrap setting. This way, if the text moves (due to editing), the graphic stays put.

In the following exercise, you change the text wrap setting for a picture.

Files needed: Chapter 8 Breton Art.docx, already open from the previous exercise

1. **In Chapter 8 Breton Art.docx, select the picture that you inserted in the previous exercise.**

   The Picture Tools Format tab becomes available.

2. **Choose Picture Tools Format⇨Wrap Text to open a menu of text wrap settings.**

   See Figure 8-5.

3. **Choose Square.**

4. **Drag the picture upward and drop it at the left margin so that it top-aligns with the top of the first body paragraph, as shown in Figure 8-6.**

Figure 8-5

For extra practice, try each of the other Wrap Text settings and compare their results. You don't have to select each of the settings; just pointing at a setting shows a preview of it in the document.

The photo currently in the document is rectangular, so you don't see any difference among some of the settings. To understand the differences among them, you must use a piece of clip art with a transparent background for your experiments.

Breton Avenue Flower Emporium

Come See What's Blooming!

week at Breton Avenue Flower Emporium, we are featuring holiday plants and flowers including fragrant pine and spruce wreaths, poinsettias, and amaryllis, all at 10% off. As an added bonus, when you buy two or more items, you'll enjoy an extra 5% off, plus free delivery within the metro area.

If you are not yet a member of the Breton Blooms Flower Club, sign up today to receive special offers via e-mail, plus a free flower arrangement on your birthday each year.

Figure 8-6

5. Press Delete to delete the picture.

6. If needed, reposition the insertion point at the beginning of the first body paragraph.

7. Using the Online Pictures command, locate and insert a poinsettia clip art image (a drawing, not a photograph) that has a white (transparent) background.

You learned about the Online Pictures command earlier, in the section "Finding and inserting pictures from the web."

8. Choose Picture Tools Format⇨Wrap Text and choose Square.

The text wraps around the clip art with a rectangular border, as shown in Figure 8-7.

EXTRA INFO

Notice the icon next to the selected picture that looks like an arch? You can click that button to open a floating version of the Wrap Text button's menu, as an alternative to clicking the Text Wrap button on the Ribbon.

Breton Avenue Flower Emporium

Come See What's Blooming!

week at Breton Avenue Flower Emporium, we are featuring holiday plants and flowers including fragrant pine and spruce wreaths, poinsettias, and amaryllis, all at 10% off. As an added bonus, when you buy two or more items, you'll enjoy an extra 5% off, plus free delivery within the metro area.

If you are not yet a member of the Breton Blooms Flower Club, sign up today to receive special offers via e-mail, plus a free flower arrangement on your birthday each year.

Figure 8-7

9. **Click the Wrap Text button again and choose Tight.**

The text wraps around the image itself, not its rectangular frame; see Figure 8-8. If the text does not wrap around the image, try a different clip art image; the one you chose might not have a transparent background, even though it looks like it does.

If any stray bits of text appear below and to the left of the image, you can fix the stray text by adjusting the image's wrap points, as explained next.

Text flows into the image's rectangular frame.

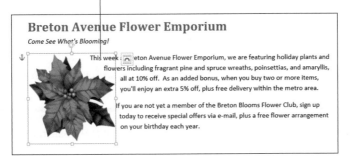

Figure 8-8

10. **Click the Wrap Text button again and choose Edit Wrap Points.**

Black squares and a dotted red outline appear around the clip art image.

These usually invisible points determine where the text is allowed to flow when text is set to Tight (that is, to wrap tightly around the image). See Figure 8-9.

11. **If needed, drag one or more of the black squares outward to block the space where the stray text appears so that it can't flow there anymore.**

12. **Click away from the image to deselect it and finalize the change in its wrap points.**

13. **Save the changes to the document.**

Leave the document open for the next exercise.

Drag a black square to adjust the way text flows into the image background.

Figure 8-9

Moving a picture

You can move a picture by dragging it where you want it to go. The way a picture moves when you drag it varies depending on the text wrap setting you've chosen for the picture:

> ✔ **If the default setting of In Line with Text is in effect,** you can drag a picture only to a spot where you can also drag text:
>
> • Within existing paragraphs
>
> • Before or after existing paragraphs
>
> However, you can't place a picture outside of the document margins or below the end-of-document marker.
>
> ✔ **If any other text wrapping setting is in effect,** you can drag a picture anywhere on the page.

You can also move a picture by specifying an exact position for it. To do so, use the Layout dialog box or one of the presets in the Position drop-down list on the Format tab under Picture Tools.

In the following exercise, you move a picture.

Files needed: Chapter 8 Breton Art.docx, already open from the previous exercise

1. **In Chapter 8 Breton Art.docx, select the picture that you worked with in the previous exercise.**

2. **Choose Picture Tools Format⇨ Position button to open a menu of positions. Choose the position that shows the picture in the upper-right corner of the document.**

    See Figure 8-10.

3. **Drag the picture downward so that its top aligns with the top of the first body paragraph.**

Figure 8-10

4. **Click the Position button again and choose More Layout Options.**

    The Layout dialog box opens with the Position tab displayed.

5. **In the Horizontal section, click Absolute Position, and then in the Absolute Position text box, enter** 5.

6. **In the Vertical section, in the Absolute Position text box, enter** 1.

Figure 8-11 shows the dialog box with these settings.

Figure 8-11

7. **Click OK to close the dialog box.**

The picture's position is adjusted according to the settings you entered.

But what if you add or delete text in the document so the text that's next to the picture now might not later be? What if you want the picture to move with the text? The following steps show how to set that up.

8. **Click the Position button and choose More Layout Options to reopen the Layout dialog box.**

9. **In the Vertical section, for the Absolute Position setting, change the value to 0" and change the Below setting to Paragraph.**

10. **Make sure that the Move Object with Text check box is selected.**

Figure 8-12 shows the dialog box with these settings.

Figure 8-12

11. **Click OK.**

12. **Click at the beginning of the paragraph that contains the document subheading ("Come see . . .") and press Enter twice.**

Notice that the picture moves with the paragraph to which it is adjacent.

13. **Press Backspace twice to delete the extra paragraphs just created.**

14. **Save the changes to the document.**

Leave the document open for the next exercise.

Resizing a picture

You can resize a picture by dragging its selection handles or by specifying an exact height and width for the picture from the Layout dialog box.

TIP

Most image types maintain the aspect ratio automatically if you drag a corner selection handle. If the aspect ratio doesn't stay constant when you drag a corner selection handle, hold down Shift as you drag to force it to do so.

WARNING!

Raster images look fuzzy if you enlarge them past their original size. That's one advantage of vector images: They remain crisp and sharp at any size.

LINGO

When you resize a picture, its **aspect ratio** can change. The aspect ratio is the proportion of width to height. A photo may not look right if you don't maintain the aspect ratio; clip art is less likely to suffer from small differences in the ratio. When you drag a corner selection handle, the aspect ratio is maintained; when you drag a side selection handle, it is not.

In the following exercise, you resize a picture.

Files needed: Chapter 8 Breton Art.docx, already open from the previous exercise

1. **In Chapter 8 Breton Art.docx, select the clip art image that you worked with in the previous exercise if it isn't already selected.**

2. **Hover the mouse pointer over the lower-left selection handle.**

   The mouse pointer becomes a double-headed diagonal arrow, as shown in Figure 8-13.

3. **Drag out and downward, enlarging the image by about ½ inch.**

   Use the onscreen ruler to gauge the distance. If the ruler does not appear, mark the Ruler check box on the View tab.

4. **Right-click the picture and choose Size and Position.**

   The Layout dialog box opens with the Size tab displayed.

5. **In the Height section, set the Absolute setting to 2".**

   The Width automatically changes because the aspect ratio is locked. See Figure 8-14. Depending on the image you are working with, the width may not be the same as the height, as it is in Figure 8-14.

Mouse pointer

Figure 8-13

Figure 8-14

6. **Click OK.**

7. **Save the changes to the document and close it.**

Leave Word open for the next exercise.

Making Basic Edits to a Picture

The original picture you insert in a Word document is just a starting point; you can modify that picture in a variety of ways to create special effects and to improve the picture's appearance. For example, you can adjust the picture's brightness and contrast, apply a color wash to it, and/or apply artistic effects to the picture that give it interesting new looks, such as making a photo look like a pencil sketch or a watercolor painting.

Adjusting brightness and contrast

If a photo suffers from being too light or too dark, you can make adjustments in Word that may help it. If a picture looks washed-out and faded, increasing its contrast may enhance it. You can also choose to sharpen or soften an image.

LINGO

Brightness refers to the overall lightness or darkness of the image, whereas **contrast** refers to the difference between the light and dark areas of a picture.

In the following exercise, you adjust the brightness, contrast, and sharpness of a picture.

Files needed: Chapter 8 Sycamore.docx

1. **In Word, open Chapter 8 Sycamore and save it as Chapter 8 Sycamore Photo.**

2. **Select the photo and then choose Picture Tools Format⇨Corrections to open a menu of samples (see Figure 8-15).**

Figure 8-15

3. **Point the mouse at several of the samples and observe the preview on the picture; then in the Brightness and Contrast section, choose the Brightness 0, Contrast +20% sample (third sample in the fourth row of the Brightness/Contrast section).**

4. **Click the Corrections button again to reopen the menu and in the Sharpen/Soften section, click the Sharpen 25% sample (fourth sample in the first row).**

5. **Save the changes to the document.**

Leave the document open for the next exercise.

Adjusting colors

You can make adjustments — subtle or dramatic — to a picture's colors from within Word. You can adjust the color saturation and the color tone. The color tone is described by "temperature" in Office applications, with lower numbers being more blue (think: frozen) and higher numbers being more orange (think: heated like a flame). For example, a strongly blue tone would be 4700K, and a strongly orange tone would be 11200K. You can also make an image grayscale or black-and-white, or apply a color wash, which makes the image monochrome (like grayscale) but with some other color than gray.

LINGO

Color saturation is the vividness of the color. **Color tone** is the subtle change in the tint of the image (red, green, or blue). **Color wash** is an effect that changes an image to a monochrome version with the chosen color as the single color that comprises it.

In the following exercise, you modify a photo's colors.

Files needed: Chapter 8 Sycamore Photo.docx, open from the preceding exercise

1. **In the Chapter 8 Sycamore Photo document, select the picture if it's not already selected.**

2. **Choose Picture Tools Format⇨Color.**

   A palette of color change options appears. See Figure 8-16.

Figure 8-16

3. Point to several of the options, and observe their effect on the image behind the open menu; then in the Color Tone section on the Color button's menu, choose Temperature: 5900K.

4. Click the Color button again, and in the Recolor section of its menu, choose Olive Green, Accent Color 3 Dark.

   The picture appears as a monochrome image in olive green.

5. Click the Color button again, and in the Recolor section of its menu, click the full-color sample (No Recolor) to return the image to multicolor.

6. Save the changes to the document.

Leave the document open for the next exercise.

Applying artistic effects

Many effects are designed to make a photograph appear as if it were drawn or painted by an artist.

In the following exercise, you apply artistic effects to a photo.

Files needed: Chapter 8 Sycamore Photo.docx, open from the preceding exercise

1. In the Chapter 8 Sycamore Photo document, select the picture if it's not already selected.

2. Choose Picture Tools Format⇨Artistic Effects.

   A palette of effect options appears. See Figure 8-17.

3. Point at several effects to see them applied to the image and then choose Pencil Sketch.

   The image's appearance takes on the qualities of a pencil sketch, as shown in Figure 8-18.

4. Save the file and close it.

Leave Word open for the next exercise.

> **LINGO**
>
> An **artistic effect** is a transformation that gives the image an altered appearance in some way. For example, some of the artistic effects include Pencil Grayscale, Line Drawing, and Watercolor Sponge.

Figure 8-17

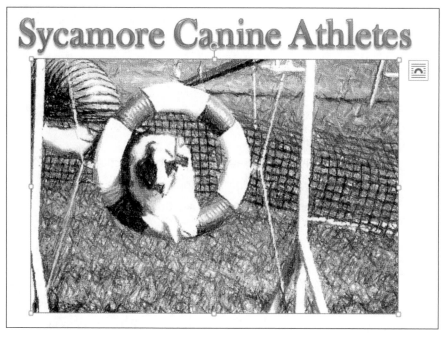

Figure 8-18

Drawing Lines and Shapes

In addition to importing other people's images, you can also draw your own via the Shapes tool in Word. By combining and formatting shapes, you can create simple illustrations and annotate other artwork with lines and shapes that call attention to certain areas.

Word doesn't differentiate between lines and shapes in its drawing tools: They're all generically called *shapes.* Therefore, when this book refers to shapes, it also includes lines.

The lines and shapes that you draw in Word are vector graphics, which means they can be drawn at any size, and moved, sized, and formatted freely after their initial placement. Drawn shapes are similar to clip art images in most ways; most of the formatting you can apply to a clip art image, you can also apply to drawn lines and shapes.

The drawing tools in Office applications are quite rudimentary, and you may find it difficult to create complex artwork using them. You can use other applications to create your artwork and then import the finished images into Office applications.

Drawing shapes

To draw a shape, use the Shapes command to open a palette of shapes and then click the one you want to draw. Then either click or drag in the Word document to create the chosen line or shape.

So which is it — click or drag? Either one will work, but they produce different results. If you click in the document, a shape of default dimensions appears. You can then resize and format it as you like. If you drag in the document, you can control the shape's dimensions by the amount you drag vertically and horizontally.

Certain shapes, such as circles and squares, are the same height and width by default, but if you drag to create them, you can distort their original aspect ratios to make ovals and rectangles. If you want to *constrain* a shape to its default aspect ratio as you draw it, hold down the Shift key while you drag.

In the following exercise, you draw some lines and shapes to create a simple picture.

Files needed: None

1. **Press Ctrl+N to start a new blank document in Word and save it as Chapter 8 Drawings.**

2. **Choose Insert⇨Shapes, and on the menu that appears, examine the available categories of shapes and the individual shapes within each one (see Figure 8-19).**

3. **In the Rectangles section, choose Rounded Rectangle.**

4. **Click anywhere on the document to place a 1-inch rounded square and then drag a side selection handle outward to increase the shape's width to 2 inches.**

5. **Choose Insert⇨Shapes again and then choose the isosceles triangle.**

6. **Hold down the Shift key and drag on the document to the right of the rectangle to create a triangle that is 1.5-inches wide at its base.**

Figure 8-19

Holding down Shift maintains the original aspect ratio of the shape.

7. **Choose Insert⇨Shapes again, and in the Lines section, choose Curve.**

8. **Move the mouse pointer to the document and then follow these steps to place the curve:**

    a. Click below the rectangle to place the beginning of the line.

    b. Move the mouse pointer about 1 inch down and 1.5 inches to the right of the original point, and then click again to place the center of the curve.

    c. Move the mouse pointer 1 inch up and 1.5 inches to the right of the previous point, and then double-click to end the drawing of the curve.

Figure 8-20 shows the drawings at this point. Your curve may look different from the one shown.

9. **Select the curve and press the Delete key to remove it.**

10. **Choose Insert⇨Shapes again, and in the Stars and Banners section, choose Up Ribbon.**

11. **Drag to draw a ribbon below the remaining shapes, approximately 5.5 inches wide and 0.5 inch high.**

12. **Save the document.**

Leave the document open for the next exercise.

Figure 8-20

Choosing a shape outline and shape fill

For a shape to be seen, it needs to have an outline, a fill, or both. By default, shapes you draw have both. The default fill color comes from the color scheme that's in use; it's the Accent 1 color (the fifth color from the left in the color palette).

The shape outline, if present, has a color, a weight (thickness), and a style (such as solid, dotted, or dashed). You can control all those options from the Drawing Tools Format tab.

Any shape (except a line) can also have a fill. This fill can be any of the following:

- ✔ A solid color
- ✔ A texture
- ✔ A pattern, such as a checkerboard or pinstripe
- ✔ A gradient
- ✔ A picture

LINGO

A **fill** is an inside color or pattern for a shape, whereas an **outline** is a colored border around the outside of a shape.

LINGO

A **texture** is a repeating graphic that makes the fill look like a certain type of surface, such as marble, wood, or newsprint. A **gradient** is a gradual blending from one color to another.

Lines don't have a fill. Their appearance is controlled by their Shape Outline setting.

In addition to the standard outline and fill choices, you can also apply Shape Effects, such as beveled edges, glow, shadows, reflection, and 3-D rotation, to drawn shapes. By combining different shapes, fills, and borders, you can create some very interesting effects.

As a shortcut to object formatting, you can apply one of the Shape Styles, available from the Drawing Tools Format tab.

In the following exercise, you format some shapes.

Files needed: Chapter 8 Drawings.docx, open from the preceding exercise

1. **In the Chapter 8 Drawings document, select the rounded rectangle.**

2. **On the Drawing Tools Format tab, click the More button in the Shape Styles group, opening the palette of shape styles, and then click the Intense Effect — Orange, Accent 2 style.**

   The style is applied to the rounded rectangle.

3. **Select the triangle; then choose Drawing Tools Format⇨Shape Fill and click the Yellow standard color.**

4. **Choose Drawing Tools Format⇨Shape Outline and click the Orange standard color.**

5. **Choose Drawing Tools Format⇨Shape Outline⇨Weight and click the ¼ point weight.**

6. **Choose Drawing Tools Format⇨ Shape Effects⇨Glow⇨More Glow Colors and then click the Orange standard color.**

   The triangle and rectangle resemble Figure 8-21 at this point.

Figure 8-21

7. **Select the banner shape; then choose Drawing Tools Format⇨Shape Fill⇨Texture⇨White Marble.**

8. Choose Drawing Tools Format⇨Shape Outline⇨No Outline.

9. Choose Drawing Tools Format⇨Shape Fill⇨Gradient⇨More Gradients.

The Format Shape task pane opens.

10. Select the Gradient Fill option if it's not already selected.

11. From the Preset Gradients drop-down list, choose Medium Gradient, Accent 4 (the gold gradient in the third row); from the Type drop-down list, choose Rectangular; and from the Direction drop-down list, choose From Bottom Right Corner.

12. Close the task pane.

13. Choose Drawing Tools Format⇨ Shape Outline and then click the Orange standard color.

The banner looks like Figure 8-22.

Figure 8-22

14. Save the changes to the document.

Leave the document open for the next exercise.

Rotating and modifying a shape, and adding text

Each shape, when selected, has a small green selection handle at its top. This is a *rotation handle;* you can drag it to rotate the shape. You can also rotate a shape by exactly 90 degrees with the Rotate button (on the Drawing Tools Format tab), or rotate it by a precise amount in the Format Shape dialog box.

Some shapes also have one or more yellow squares on them when selected. They look like extra selection handles. These squares are for modifying the shape's dimensions; you can drag one of the yellow squares to change a certain part of the shape. For example, on a block arrow, separate squares change the size of the arrow head and the arrow shaft.

To add text to a shape, just select the shape and begin typing. The text is placed in the center of the shape. The shape is a type of text box, and can be formatted in much the same way as any other text box.

In the following exercise, you rotate and modify some shapes.

*Files needed: Chapter 8 Drawings.docx, open from
the preceding exercise*

1. **In the Chapter 8 Drawings document, select the triangle and then choose Drawing Tools Format⇨Rotate Objects⇨Rotate Right 90° (see Figure 8-23).**

2. **Choose Drawing Tools Format⇨Rotate Objects⇨Rotate Right 90° again to rotate the triangle another 90 degrees.**

3. **Choose Drawing Tools Format⇨Rotate Objects⇨Flip Vertical.**

   The triangle returns to its original appearance.

Figure 8-23

REMEMBER

Flipping is not the same as rotating for some shapes. It happens to have the same effect for this triangle, but if you try it on an irregular shape, such as Explosion 2, you will see the difference.

4. **Drag the rotation handle on the triangle to rotate it so that the tip of the triangle (the point closest to the rotation handle) points to the right.**

5. **Right-click the triangle and choose Format Shape.**

   The Format Shape task pane opens.

6. **Click the Effects icon (the pentagon) at the top of the task pane.**

7. **Click 3-D Rotation to expand those options.**

8. **In the Z Rotation text box, type 270 (see Figure 8-24) so that the shape is rotated for the tip to point downward. Close the task pane when finished.**

9. **Click the banner shape and then drag the leftmost yellow square on its border to the left as far as possible, increasing the middle section of the banner.**

10. **Drag the yellow square on the bottom middle of the shape upward as far as possible, shrinking the height of the middle section of the banner.**

11. **Double-click in the banner and type ACME Corporation.**

Tip of triangle points down   Z Rotation of 270

Figure 8-24

12. **Select the text you just typed; choose Home⇨Font Color and choose black for the text color. Then click away from the banner to view it.**

ACME Corporation

Figure 8-25

The banner looks like Figure 8-25.

13. **Save the changes to the document.**

Leave the document open for the next exercise.

Stacking and grouping shapes

Single shapes may sometimes be useful in a document, but the real power of the Shapes feature can be found by combining shapes to create more complex drawings and logos. You can stack the shapes on top of each other and control the order in which they appear in the stack. After you have a group of shapes arranged just the way you want them, you can then use the Group command to meld them together into one object that you can move and resize as a whole.

In the following exercise, you combine several shapes into a logo and then group them into a single object.

Files needed: Chapter 8 Drawings.docx, open from the preceding exercise

1. **In the Chapter 8 Drawings document, change the triangle's height and width to 1.75 inches each.**

   You can do this by dragging its side selection handles and using the ruler to gauge the measurement, or by displaying the Drawing Tools Format tab and entering precise measurements in the Size group.

2. **Drag the triangle on top of the rounded rectangle, and then center the triangle vertically and horizontally over the rectangle (see Figure 8-26).**

   Figure 8-26

3. **With the triangle selected, choose Drawing Tools Format⟿Send Backward to move the triangle behind the rectangle.**

4. **Choose Drawing Tools Format⟿Bring Forward⟿Bring to Front.**

   The triangle moves forward again, in front of the rectangle.

5. **Drag the banner on top of the other shapes, and then center it vertically and horizontally.**

   The triangle obscures the banner because the triangle is set to be the front object.

6. **With the banner selected, click Bring Forward until the banner is fully visible.**

   The logo looks like Figure 8-27.   **Figure 8-27**

7. **Hold down the Shift key and click each of the three shapes, selecting them all; then choose Drawing Tools Format⇨Group Objects⇨Group.**

The shapes are grouped into one object.

8. **Save the changes to the document and close it.**

Exit Word.

 # Summing Up

Word accepts a variety of graphics, including clip art, photographs, and drawn lines and shapes. Here are the important skills and concepts in this chapter:

- ✔ The Online Pictures feature, which you access by choosing Insert⇨Online Pictures, searches for clips in Microsoft's extensive online collection or using a Bing image search.

- ✔ When you search for images, you can specify one or more keywords.

- ✔ A picture's text wrap setting determines whether it will be an inline image or will interact with surrounding text (and in what manner).

- ✔ To move a picture, drag it with the mouse. You can also specify an exact position for it in the Layout dialog box.

- ✔ To resize a picture, drag one of its selection handles. Drag a corner to resize it proportionally (that is, maintaining its aspect ratio).

- ✔ The Picture Tools Format tab contains buttons for modifying a picture in several ways, including adjusting its brightness, contrast, and sharpness, and changing its color.

- ✔ You can apply artistic effects to a picture from the Picture Tools Format tab. These effects make a photo seem like it has been drawn or painted by hand.

- ✔ Draw your own lines and shapes by choosing Insert⇨Shapes. You can then format these graphics via the Drawing Tools Format tab.

- ✔ The circular arrow symbol at the top of a selected graphic is its rotation handle; drag it to rotate the graphic.

- ✔ On a drawn line or shape, the yellow square(s), if present, are shape-changing handles; drag one of them to modify the shape.

- ✔ To group shapes, select them and then choose Drawing Tools Format⇨ Group Objects⇨Group.

Try-it-yourself lab

For more practice with the features covered in this chapter, try the following exercise on your own:

1. **Start Word and begin creating a flyer that advertises a yard sale. Type the appropriate text, including a location, the date and time, and a list of items to be sold.**

2. **Find and insert two pieces of clip art that would be appropriate for this flyer.**

3. **Set the text wrapping on the clip art so that the text wraps around the clips. Then position and size the clips attractively.**

4. **Enhance the flyer further by drawing at least two shapes on the flyer and formatting them to match the look of the rest of the flyer.**

 For example, you might use starbursts or arrows to call attention to important text.

5. **Save your document as Chapter 8 Flyer.**

6. **Close the document and exit Word.**

Know this tech talk

aspect ratio: The proportion of height to width of an image.

brightness: The overall lightness or darkness of an image.

clip art: Generic, predrawn artwork, available from third-party sources or from Microsoft's Office.com collection.

color saturation: The vividness of the color in an image.

color tone: The tint of an image.

color wash: An effect applied to an image that makes it monochrome but with some other color than gray.

contrast: The difference between the light and dark areas of an image.

fill: The color of the inside of a shape.

inline image: A picture that's placed within the document's paragraph structure and is treated as a character of text.

outline: The color and other properties of the outside border of a shape, or of a line.

pixel: An individual dot or data point in a raster graphic.

raster graphic: A type of graphic that defines the color of each pixel (or dot) that makes up the image individually.

text wrap: The setting that determines how the surrounding text interacts with an image, if it isn't an inline image.

vector graphic: A type of graphic that defines each line or fill with a math formula.

Chapter 9
Managing Correspondence

✔ Word can print envelopes that *match your business correspondence in font and style.*

✔ Saving a return address enables you to *create other envelopes later without retyping* the return address.

✔ Mail merge enables you to *combine a list of addresses with a form for labels, envelopes, or letters.*

✔ Sorting the records in a mail merge allows them to *print in the order you* specify.

✔ Filtering the records in a mail merge enables you to *exclude certain records from displaying or printing.*

his chapter covers creating special-purpose documents, such as envelopes, and creating mail merges that enable you to customize multiple copies of an envelope, label, or document from a separately stored data list. You learn how to set up basic merges and how to sort and filter a mail merge data source.

Creating Envelopes

Envelopes are the natural companions of business and personal letters. Most of the time, when you print a letter, you also want an envelope for it. You can address the envelope by hand, of course, but printing an envelope is quick and easy in Word.

One nice thing about the Envelopes feature in Word is that it can automatically extract the mailing address from the letter, so you don't have to retype it. The Envelopes feature also stores your return address and recalls it for you each time you print an envelope.

An envelope has a different paper size and orientation than a business letter, so how does Word manage to store them both in the same file? Word creates a section break between the letter and the envelope. Each section, such as headers/footers, watermarks, page numbers, and more, can have its own settings that would normally apply to the entire document. To find details about using sections to store different page settings in one document, see Chapter 6.

Adding an envelope to a document

In the following exercise, you add an envelope to a document.

Files needed: Chapter 9 Letter.docx

1. **Open the Chapter 9 Letter document and save it as Chapter 9 Letter Envelope.**

2. **Choose Mailings➪Envelopes.**

   The Envelopes and Labels dialog box opens. Word attempts to fill in the correct address in the Delivery Address box, but in this case, it fails; it fills in the bulleted list instead of the mailing address.

3. **Click Cancel to close the dialog box.**

4. **Select the recipient name and address in the letter (*Mr. Charlie Lutz, 475 E. Main St., Carmel, IN 46025*) and then choose Mailings➪ Envelopes again.**

   This time Word fills in the address correctly.

5. **Type your own return address, or make one up, in the Return Address box (see Figure 9-1), click Add to Document (or Change Document), and if prompted to save the return address as the default, click Yes.**

   A new section is created at the beginning of the document, and the envelope is placed there. Notice in Figure 9-2 that the new section has a different paper size, orientation, and margins than the letter.

Return address

EXTRA INFO

In the future, this address will be fill automatically. If you use the return addre rent envelope but m: it in the future, you Omit check box in the Envelopes and Labels dialog box. If you don't want to use the address anymore permanently, delete it from the Return Address box.

Click Add to Document to create an envelope in the document.

Figure 9-1

Envelope

Letter

Figure 9-2

To understand how the document can have two different page sizes, switch to Draft view. Notice the section break between the two pages. Switch back to Print Layout view when finished.

Leave the document open for the next exercise.

Changing the envelope size

There are many different shapes and sizes of envelopes, and Word can accommodate any of them. However, you must tell Word the dimensions of the envelope you're using so that when you're ready to print, Word can pass the correct size of your envelope to your printer.

In the following exercise, you change the size of an envelope definition stored in a Word document.

Files needed: Chapter 9 Letter Envelope.docx, open from the preceding exercise

1. **In the Chapter 9 Letter Envelope document, choose Mailings⇨Envelopes to reopen the Envelopes and Labels dialog box and then click the Options button.**

   The Envelope Options dialog box opens. See Figure 9-3.

2. **From the Envelope Size drop-down list, choose Monarch, and then click OK to return to the Envelopes and Labels dialog box.**

3. **Click the Change Document button.**

   The envelope size changes in the document.

4. **Using the same procedure as in Steps 1 through 3, change the envelope size to Size 10.**

   Figure 9-3

Leave the document open for the next exercise.

Printing an envelope

To print an envelope, feed an envelope into your printer and then print the section of the document that contains the envelope. You can either do this manually (by choosing File⇨Print and then selecting only page 1 to print) or you can reopen the Envelopes and Labels dialog box and print from there, in which case only the envelope (not the letter) prints.

In the following exercise, you print an envelope.

Files needed: Chapter 9 Letter Envelope.docx, open from the preceding exercise

1. **Choose Mailings⇨Envelopes to reopen the Envelopes and Labels dialog box (see Figure 9-4).**

Figure 9-4

2. **Feed an envelope into your printer and then click the Print button in the dialog box.**

   The envelope prints.

3. **Save and close the document.**

Leave Word open for the next exercise.

If printing the envelope doesn't go as you expected — say, it prints on the wrong side, or it's not lined up correctly — you might need to try again and change the orientation at which you feed it into the printer. For example, you might need to feed the envelope sideways, rotated 180 degrees, or upside down.

To avoid wasting an envelope, do a test print with plain paper. Draw an arrow on a piece of paper, and put it into your printer's paper tray, face up, arrow facing in. Then print what will appear on your envelope on that paper. The relationship between the printout and the arrow can tell you how to orient the envelopes you feed in. For example, if the arrow is on the reverse side from the printing, you know that envelopes need to be fed into the printer flap up.

Performing a Mail Merge

Big companies use mail merge to mail customized advertisements, but it's not just for businesses. Home users can take advantage of mail merge for Christmas card mailing labels, party invitations, club newsletters, and more.

Performing a mail merge is a three-step process:

1. Create (or identify) the data source.

2. Create the main document and then insert the merge codes in it.

3. Perform the merge operation between the data source and the main document.

The data source must be a *delimited file*. In other words, there has to be some consistent way that it distinguishes between one column or row of data and the next. Here are some possible data source types:

> **LINGO**
>
> A **mail merge** combines a data list, usually of names and addresses (that is, mailing information), with a form letter, a label, or an envelope template to produce customized copies of the letter for each person.

> **LINGO**
>
> The **data source** is the file that contains the names to be merged, whereas the **main document** is the file that contains the text that will be the same for each copy, plus the codes to link to the data source.

 ✓ **Excel or Word table:** If the data source is an Excel spreadsheet, each type of information is in a separate column, as shown in Figure 9-5. The same goes if the data source is a Word table.

	A	B	C	D	E
1	Name	Address	City	State	ZIP
2	Jan Smith	1847 Ponting Street	Avon	IN	46872
3	Karen Clark	4827 South Westover	Carmel	IN	46208
4	Sylvia Sharp	522 Ridge Way	Mcon	IL	62544
5	George Colvin	967 State Road 26	Anderson	IN	46119

Figure 9-5

 ✓ **Plain text:** If the data source is a plain text file, each column is delimited (separated) by a specific character, such as a tab or a comma. When a delimited text file uses commas, it's a Comma Separated Values, or CSV, file. The example in Figure 9-6 uses a comma.

```
                        Untitled - Notepad       – □ ×
File  Edit  Format  View  Help
Name,Address,City,State,ZIP
Jan Smith,1847 Ponting Street,Avon,IN,46872
Karen Clark,4827 South Westover,Carmel,IN,46208
Sylvia Sharp,522 Ridge Way,Mcon,IL,62544
George Colvin,967 State Road 26,Anderson,IN,46119
```

Figure 9-6

 ✓ **Outlook:** If the data source is an Outlook Contacts list, each type of information is in a separate field.

 ✓ **Word list:** If you don't have a data source already, choose Mailings⇨Select Recipients⇨Type New List to create one with the Type New List feature in Word.

A data file shouldn't contain anything except the data (and perhaps a single row of field labels, as in Figure 9-6 with Name, Address, City, State, and ZIP). Don't use any blank rows or titles at the top of the page because that confuses the Mail Merge utility. Check your data file to remove extraneous rows before using the file as your mail merge source.

After preparing the data file, you set up the main document. You can either create the main document from scratch, or you can start with an existing document and convert it to be a mail merge main document. The main document consists of regular text plus codes that show where the merge fields should be inserted. Figure 9-7 shows an example.

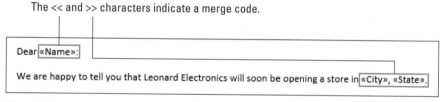

The << and >> characters indicate a merge code.

Dear «Name»:

We are happy to tell you that Leonard Electronics will soon be opening a store in «City», «State».

Figure 9-7

Then, as the final step in the merge process, you bring together the two pieces. You can do so either by sending the results directly to the printer or by creating a new document that contains the merge, which you can then edit as needed and then print.

Creating mail-merged letters

Letters are one of the most common mail-merged document types. Typically the merge fields are used to generate the mailing address. In some letters, fields are also used to customize the letter itself (refer to Figure 9-7).

Word 2013 provides two time-saving code blocks, <<AddressBlock>> and <<GreetingLine>>. You find buttons for these codes on the Mailings tab.

The <<AddressBlock>> code sets up a standard mailing address for you, or you can insert individual codes to create the mailing address block yourself. For example, the following are equivalent:

<<AddressBlock>>   <<Name>>

                           <<Address>>

                           <<City>>,

                           <<State>>

                           <<ZIP>>

Word also provides a <<GreetingLine>> code block that inserts a greeting, such as *Dear* <<*Title*>> <<*LastName*>>. You can customize the greeting line code to use any combination of titles, first names, and last names.

> The following exercise doesn't use the greeting line code because the data file doesn't have separate fields for first and last names, and the <<GreetingLine>> code works best when those names are separate.

In this exercise, you create mail-merged letters.

Files needed: Chapter 9 Main.docx and Chapter 9 Data.xlsx

1. **Open Chapter 9 Main and save it as Chapter 9 Main Merge.**

2. **Choose Mailings⇨Start Mail Merge⇨Letters.**

3. **Choose Mailings⇨Select Recipients⇨Use an Existing List.**

   The Select Data Source dialog box opens. See Figure 9-8.

Figure 9-8

4. **Navigate to the folder containing the data files for this chapter. Select Chapter 9 Data.xlsx and click Open.**

   The Select Table dialog box opens, prompting you to choose which worksheet you want to use.

5. **In the Select Table dialog box, make sure Sheet1$ is selected and click OK.**

6. **Move the insertion point to the line immediately below the date and then choose Mailings⇨Address Block.**

   The Insert Address Block dialog box opens. See Figure 9-9.

TIP

If the sample in the Preview area is not right, click the Match Fields button and specify which fields should be associated with which parts of the address block.

Figure 9-9

7. **Confirm that the address in the Preview area looks correctly formed and then click OK to accept the default settings.**

   An `<<AddressBlock>>` code appears in the document.

8. **Press Enter to start a new line after the `<<AddressBlock>>` code and then type Dear and press the space bar once.**

9. **On the Mailings tab, click the down arrow below Insert Merge Field, and on the menu that appears click Name.**

   A `<<Name>>` code is inserted.

10. **Type a comma after the code and then click to move the insertion point immediately before the word *store* in the first paragraph.**

11. **Click the down arrow under the Insert Merge Field button again, and click City.**

    A <<City>> code is inserted at the insertion point.

12. **Press the space bar once to add a space after the code.**

    The letter looks like Figure 9-10.

Address block   City field

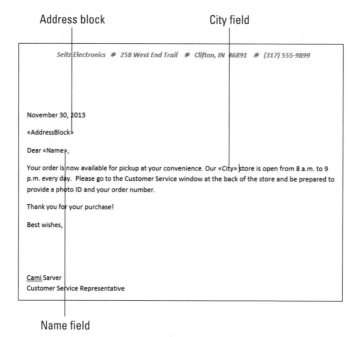

Seitz Electronics ✳ *258 West End Trail* ✳ *Clifton, IN 46891* ✳ *(317) 555-9899*

November 30, 2013

«AddressBlock»

Dear «Name»,

Your order is now available for pickup at your convenience. Our «City» store is open from 8 a.m. to 9 p.m. every day. Please go to the Customer Service window at the back of the store and be prepared to provide a photo ID and your order number.

Thank you for your purchase!

Best wishes,

Cami Sarver
Customer Service Representative

Name field

Figure 9-10

13. **Choose Mailings⇨Preview Results.**

    The first letter appears as it will be printed. Notice that extra space is between the lines of the address block.

14. **Select all the lines of the address block on the previewed letter and then choose Home⇨Line and Paragraph Spacing⇨Remove Space after Paragraph (see Figure 9-11). Click away from the selection to deselect it when finished.**

    This takes care of the spacing problem for all letters in the merge file.

Line and Paragraph Spacing button

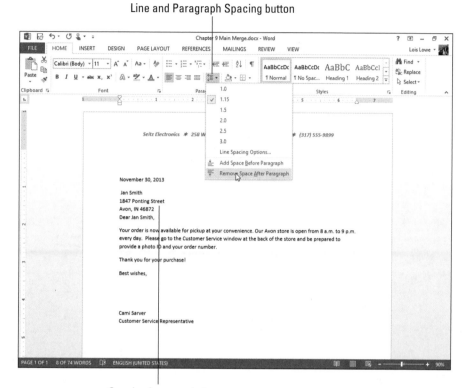

Spacing is corrected.

Figure 9-11

15. **Click at the end of the last line of the address block and press Enter once, creating an extra line of space between the address and the greeting.**

16. **Choose Mailings⇨Next Record to see a preview of the next letter (see Figure 9-12).**

> To make the letters look better, you could center them vertically on the page, as you learn to do in Chapter 6.

Next Record button

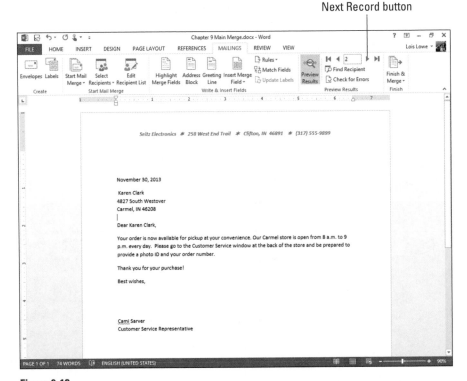

Figure 9-12

17. **Keep clicking Next Record until you have seen all the records and then choose Mailings⇨Finish & Merge⇨Edit Individual Documents.**

    The Merge to New Document dialog box opens.

18. **Click OK to merge all the copies into one document.**

    A new document — Letters1 — opens.

19. **Scroll through the new document to check the letters; then close it without saving changes to it.**

20. **Save your changes to the Chapter 9 Main Merge file and then close it.**

Leave Word open for the next exercise.

Creating mail-merged labels

Another type of mail merge involves printing on sticky-backed labels, which you can then pull apart and use for package mailing, name tags, or any other purpose you might use labels for.

The mail merge process is much the same for labels, except that you specify a label type and size and then Word creates a table that mimics the labels. The merge fields are placed into the upper-left corner cell of the table and copied into the other cells.

In this exercise, you create mail-merged labels.

Files needed: Chapter 9 Data.xlsx

1. **In Word, press Ctrl+N to start a new blank document, save it as Chapter 9 Labels.docx, and then choose Mailings⇨Start Mail Merge⇨Labels.**

   The Label Options dialog box appears.

2. **From the Label Vendors drop-down list, choose Avery US Letter; in the Product Number list, choose 5160 Easy Peel Address Labels (see Figure 9-13); click OK.**

   Figure 9-13

Almost every size and shape of label has a code on the packaging or the label sheet itself. When you create labels for your own purposes, you just match that code with one of the templates in Word. In Step 2, 5160 Easy Peel Address Labels is an example of a label code.

3. **If you don't see the gridlines of the table onscreen, choose Table Tools Layout⇨View Gridlines.**

4. **Choose Mailings⇨Select Recipients⇨Use an Existing List.**

   The Select Data Source dialog box opens (refer to Figure 9-8).

5. **Navigate to the folder containing the data files for this chapter. Select Chapter 9 Data.xlsx and click Open.**

   The Select Table dialog box opens, prompting you to choose which worksheet you'll use for the data source.

6. **In the Select Table dialog box, make sure Sheet1$ is selected and then click OK.**

   The data source is attached. In the table, <<Next Record>> codes appear in every cell except the upper-left one. See Figure 9-14.

Figure 9-14

7. **Choose Mailings⇨Address Block, and in the Insert Address Block dialog box that appears, click OK to accept the default address block settings.**

   The <<AddressBlock>> code appears only in the upper-left cell.

   For more practice, you could delete the <<AddressBlock>> code and construct your own address block manually by inserting the <<Name>> field, pressing Shift+Enter, inserting the <<Address>> field, pressing Shift+Enter, inserting the <<City>> field, typing a comma and a space, inserting the <<State>> field, typing two spaces, and inserting the <<ZIP>> field.

8. **Choose Mailings⇨Update Labels.**

   The code from the upper-left cell is copied to all the other cells.

9. **Choose Mailings⇨Preview Results.**

   The four label results appear, as shown in Figure 9-15.

Figure 9-15

10. Save the document.

Leave the document open for the next exercise.

Sorting and Filtering Mail Merge Records

If you pull data from a large database to create your mail merge or pull from a data source that includes more records than you need for your purposes, you may find it helpful to sort and/or filter the data to show only what you want, in the order you want it. In the following exercises, you sort and filter your data.

Sorting a merge data source

Sorting the records in the data source places them in alphabetical order (or numeric order) based on one or more fields. For example, you might want to print mailing labels in zip code order, or by last name.

In this exercise, you sort the records in a mail merge by zip code.

Files needed: Chapter 9 Labels.xlsx, open from the preceding exercise

1. In the Chapter 9 Labels document, choose Mailings➪Edit Recipient List.

The Mail Merge Recipients dialog box opens.

2. **Click the down-pointing arrow on the ZIP field's column header, choose Sort Ascending (see Figure 9-16), and click OK.**

The records appear in zip code order, as shown in Figure 9-17.

> **TIP**
>
> If field codes appear instead of records, choose Mailings⇨Preview Results.

> **EXTRA INFO**
>
> If you need a multilevel sort to break ties, such as sorting by last name if two records have the same zip code, click the Sort link in the Refine Recipient List section of the Mail Merge Recipients dialog box (see Figure 9-16) to set up your sort in a dialog box that allows multiple sort levels.

Figure 9-16

George Colvin	Karen Clark	Jan Smith
967 State Road 26	4827 South Westover	1847 Ponting Street
Anderson, IN 46119	Carmel, IN 46208	Avon, IN 46872
Sylvia Sharp		
522 Ridge Way		
Macon, IL 62544		

Figure 9-17

3. **Save the document.**

Leave the document open for the next exercise.

Filtering a merge data source

Filtering a data source excludes certain records (or, to look at it another way, it includes only certain records) on the basis of one or more criteria you specify. For example, you might want only addresses from a certain city or state to be included, or only those that match a list of certain cities or states.

Filtering data excludes certain records from the merge results, but does not delete the rejected data from the original copy of the data source, so you can choose later to re-include it, or include it when using that same data set for other projects.

In this exercise, you filter the records in a mail merge to show only those with certain cities.

Files needed: Chapter 9 Labels.xlsx, open from the preceding exercise

1. **Choose Mailings⇨Edit Recipient List.**

   The Mail Merge Recipients dialog box opens.

2. **Click the down-pointing arrow on the City field's column header, choose Avon (see Figure 9-18), and click OK.**

   The label preview changes to show only one label.

Figure 9-18

3. **Choose Mailings⇨Edit Recipient List.**

   The Mail Merge Recipients dialog box opens.

4. **Click the down-pointing arrow on the City field's column header and choose (All).**

   The complete list of all four records reappears. See Figure 9-19.

Figure 9-19

5. **Click the down-pointing arrow on the City field's column header and choose (Advanced).**

   The Filter and Sort dialog box opens with the Filter Records tab displayed.

6. **Choose City from the first drop-down list in the Field column; in the Compare To column, in the first text box, type** Avon **(see Figure 9-20).**

Figure 9-20

7. **In the second row, choose Or from the And drop-down list; choose City from the Field drop-down list in the second row; and in the second row in the Compare To column, type** Carmel **(see Figure 9-21).**

Figure 9-21

8. **Click OK to accept the new filtering criteria and then click OK to close the Mail Merge Recipients dialog box.**

   Two labels appear in the results: one for Avon and one for Carmel.

9. **Save the document and close it.**

Exit Word.

 Summing Up

Here are the key points from this chapter:

✓ You can include an envelope in the same document as a letter. The envelope is in a different section, which enables it to have a different page size.

✓ To add an envelope to a document, change its size, or print it, choose Mailings⇨Envelopes.

✓ Mail merges combine a main document with a database listing to create customized copies of the main document. Use the commands on the Mailings tab to set up mail merges.

✓ To choose which type of document to mail merge, choose Mailings⇨ Start Mail Merge and then choose either Letters or Labels.

✓ To select a data source for the mail merge, choose Mailings⇨Select Recipients⇨Use an Existing List.

✓ To insert fields into the main document, choose Mailings⇨Address Block for a full address block, or choose Mailings⇨Insert Merge Field to select a specific field.

✔ To sort the recipients, choose Mailings➪Edit Recipient List and then click the down arrow on one of the column headings to sort by that field.

✔ To filter the recipients, choose Mailings➪Edit Recipient List and then open the menu for the field's column header and choose what values to include or exclude.

Try-it-yourself lab

For more practice with the features covered in this chapter, try the following exercise on your own:

1. **Start a new blank document and start a Labels mail merge. Use any size label you like. Save the document as Chapter 9 Label Main.**

2. **Using your Outlook Contacts list or any delimited data file that contains names and addresses, create mailing labels that you could use to distribute your newsletter by postal mail.**

   If you don't have an appropriate data file, create one by choosing Mailings➪Select Recipients➪Type New List.

3. **Perform the mail merge to create the labels in a new document and save the new document as Chapter 9 Label Merge.**

4. **Close all documents and exit Word.**

Know this tech talk

address block: An <<AddressBlock>> code that creates a fully formed name and address for mailing in a mail merge document.

data source: The file containing the data to be used for a mail merge.

delimited: A file that uses a consistent character to separate data into multiple columns. A comma or a tab stop is commonly used as a delimiter character.

mail merge: Combining a data list with a form letter, label, or envelope template to produce customized copies.

main document: The document in a mail merge that contains the standardized text and the codes for linking to the data source.

Chapter 10
Preparing Professional Reports

- ✔ A Table of Contents *lets readers know the starting page numbers* for each heading.

- ✔ An index *provides an alphabetical listing of important terms and their page numbers.*

- ✔ Figure captions make it easier to *refer to a specific figure in the text.*

- ✔ A Table of Authorities *provides a list of legal citations in a document.*

- ✔ Footnotes and endnotes *provide background information separate from the main text.*

*W*hen preparing long documents, you might want to take advantage of some of the many features that Word has for keeping things organized across multiple pages. Here's a quick overview of the tools and how they're helpful:

- **To help readers navigate a document,** Word can generate a Table of Contents and an index.
- **If your document includes figures,** Word helps you create captions and a reference of all the figures in your document. Word's capability to auto-number figures helps you keep things numbered sequentially as you edit and move text.
- **If your document must follow certain legal conventions,** Word has features specifically for numbering lines and creating a Table of Authorities.
- **If your document has footnotes and endnotes,** Word keeps track of their numbering and placement.

TIP

To use many of these tools, you need to understand how styles and automatic page numbering work. (See Chapters 5 and 6, respectively.) Before you embed lots of figures in a long document, be sure you understand the basics of working with graphics in Word. (That's the focus of Chapter 8.)

Creating a Table of Contents

Most technical and educational books include a Table of Contents, or TOC, to help readers quickly locate specific sections. A TOC lists each heading of the document, and either lists its page number (suitable for printed copies) or provides a live hyperlink to it (suitable for online copies).

LINGO

A **Table of Contents,** or **TOC,** is a chronological list of the main headings in the document, with page numbers or hyperlinks that provide quick access to the referenced sections.

Defining heading levels

TOCs are created based on the styles in your document. Each of the built-in heading styles in Word has a specific TOC level pre-assigned to it, but you can change these.

TIP

You can also assign TOC levels to other styles as well, including styles that you wouldn't typically associate with headings. For example, you could assign a TOC level to a style you use for figure captions to include each figure caption in your TOC.

In this exercise, you modify the TOC levels for the styles used for headings in a document.

Files needed: Chapter 10 Bio.docx

1. **Open Chapter 10 Bio and save it as Chapter 10 Bio Complete.**

2. **On the Home tab, click the dialog box launcher in the Styles group.**

   The Styles pane opens.

3. **Scroll down in the document to the first heading: *Early Career.* Click to move the insertion point into it.**

   In the Styles pane, the Major style is highlighted.

4. **Point to the Major style in the Styles pane, and when a down arrow appears to its right, click the arrow to open its menu and choose Modify (see Figure 10-1).**

   The Modify Style dialog box opens.

5. **In the bottom-left corner of the dialog box, click the Format button and choose Paragraph (see Figure 10-2).**

Figure 10-1

Figure 10-2

6. In the Paragraph dialog box that appears, from the Outline Level drop-down list, choose Level 1 (see Figure 10-3), click OK to close the Paragraph dialog box, and then click OK to close the Modify Style dialog box.

7. Move the insertion point into the minor title of Birth of the Royal Australian Air Force, and then repeat Steps 4 through 6 to assign Level 2 to the Minor style.

8. Click the Close (x) button on the Styles pane to close it.

9. Save the document.

Leave the document open for the next exercise.

Figure 10-3

Generating a TOC

You can place a TOC anywhere in a document, but it's traditionally placed at the beginning, or at least near the beginning (for example, following a cover page). You have many options for generating the TOC, such as number alignment, hyperlinking, and the levels to include.

In this exercise, you generate a Table of Contents.

Files needed: Chapter 10 Bio Complete.docx, open from the preceding exercise

1. **Press Ctrl+Home to move the insertion point to the beginning of the Chapter 10 Bio Complete document.**

2. **Choose References⇨Table of Contents⇨Automatic Table 1 (see Figure 10-4).**

   A default-formatted TOC appears in the document, as shown in Figure 10-5.

3. **Press Ctrl+Z or click the Undo button on the Quick Access Toolbar to remove the TOC.**

   You re-create it via different settings next.

4. **Choose References⇨Table of Contents⇨Custom Table of Contents.**

   The Table of Contents dialog box opens.

Figure 10-4

Contents

Figure 10-5

5. **From the Formats drop-down list, choose Formal (see Figure 10-6) and then click OK.**

A differently formatted TOC appears.

Figure 10-6

6. **Save the document.**

Leave the document open for the next exercise.

Updating a TOC

When you make changes to the document, the TOC doesn't update automatically. You can refresh it at any time, however.

In this exercise, you update a Table of Contents.

Files needed: Chapter 10 Bio Complete.docx, open from the preceding exercise

1. **Scroll down to the first heading in the Chapter 10 Bio Complete document** *(Early Career)* **and edit it to** Early Life.

2. **Scroll back up to the top of the document and then, in the Table of Contents group of the References tab, choose Update Table.**

The Update Table of Contents dialog box opens.

3. **Select Update Entire Table, as shown in Figure 10-7, and then click OK.**

   The TOC updates to show the new wording.

4. **Save the document.**

Leave the document open for the next exercise.

Figure 10-7

Working with TOC styles

The text within the TOC is formatted according to special built-in TOC styles in Word. You can select a different format when creating the TOC (via the Formats drop-down list), as you did earlier in the "Generating a TOC" section. You can also fine-tune the TOC's styles by modifying the styles individually.

In this exercise, you modify a TOC style.

Files needed: Chapter 10 Bio Complete. docx, open from the preceding exercise

1. **In the TOC at the beginning of the Chapter 10 Bio Complete document, click in the first line (*Early Life*).**

2. **On the Home tab, click the dialog box launcher in the Styles group, opening the Styles pane.**

3. **In the Styles pane, scroll down to the TOC styles (see Figure 10-8).**

4. **Right-click the TOC 1 style in the Styles pane and choose Modify.**

   The Modify Style dialog box opens, as shown in Figure 10-9.

Figure 10-8

Bold button

Figure 10-9

5. Click the Bold button to turn off the Bold attribute and then click OK.

All text using that style is updated (that is, all the Level 1 text in the TOC). In Figure 10-10, notice that all the headings that use the TOC 1 style are no longer bold.

Figure 10-10

6. Click away from the TOC to deselect it and then click the Close (x) button on the Styles pane to close it.

7. Save the document.

Leave the document open for the next exercise.

Creating an Index

Creating an index would be kind of daunting without tools to help you. With Word's indexing tools, you have to mark the important words to include in your index, but Word can alphabetize the entries for you and keep track of the page numbers on which those words appear.

In other words, creating an index is a two-step process:

1. Mark the index entries in the document.

2. Compile the index.

LINGO

An **index** is an alphabetical list of important words in the document, along with page numbers in which those words are featured. Whereas a TOC helps readers find headings in the document, an index helps you find specific words and phrases.

When marking entries, each entry can be one of three types:

- A **main entry** appears in alphabetical order in the index. These are the important words that your readers might look up.

- A **subentry** appears subordinate to a main entry. Subentries are appropriate when a term makes sense only in the context of a main term. For example, if the main entry is *Civil War,* you might have a subentry of *Economic impact.*

- A **cross-reference** is a reference to a main entry. A cross-reference is useful when one term is an abbreviation of another. For example, the main entry might be *United States of America* and the cross-reference might be *USA.*

  Cross-references are also useful when a certain word that a user might be likely to look up is not the same word as is used for that topic in the book. For example, suppose you are writing about the Find feature in Word; you might list *Search* as a cross-reference to Find, in case the reader didn't know the official name of the feature.

Look at the index for this book and you will see examples of all three types.

Marking index entries

To mark entries for an index, you use the Mark Entry tool on the References tab. When you mark an index entry, Word places a hidden code in the document immediately following the word or phrase.

Marking the index entries can be a time-consuming task. Although the Mark Entry tool does have a Mark All option, which marks all instances of a word at once, the Mark All option tends to over-mark. This means your index will include incidental uses of a word rather than only the important uses, and thus make your index less useful to your readers.

To generate an index that only cites significant uses of your indexed terms, mark each index entry individually. Avoid the Mark All option except in special cases where marking every single instance of a term is desired.

Professional-quality indexes are marked by professional indexers, and a large document, such as a book, can take many days to mark.

In this exercise, you mark index entries.

Files needed: Chapter 10 Bio Complete.docx, open from the preceding exercise

1. **In the first paragraph of the Chapter 10 Bio Complete document, select the text *World War I* and then choose References⇨Mark Entry.**

   The Mark Index Entry dialog box opens. See Figure 10-11.

2. **Click the Mark All button.**

   An index entry code is inserted in the document. See Figure 10-12. Word displays hidden characters if they aren't already displayed so that the index code is visible. All other instances of *World War I* are also marked. The dialog box remains open.

You can mark instances individually, or mark them all at once, depending on whether you want every instance to be indexed. Between entries, you can close the dialog box or leave it open. If you close it and then select some text, the selected text appears in the Main Entry text box automatically.

Figure 10-11

Indexing code

trained·in·Australia,·and·went·on·to·command·Australian·and·British·fighter·units·in·World·War·
I{XE·"World·War·I"·}·A·proponent·for·air·power·independent·of·other·branches·of·the·armed·
services,·Williams·played·a·leading·role·in·the·establishment·of·the·RAAF·and·became·its·first·

Figure 10-12

3. **Click the Close button to close the dialog box and then use the same process as in Steps 1 and 2 to mark all instances of** *Royal Australian Air Force.*

   Mark All should be used sparingly because of the problems discussed earlier in this section, but Mark All is appropriate in cases where the reader may be interested in finding every mention of a term.

   Leave the dialog box open when finished.

4. **In the first paragraph, select the text** *RAAF.* **Then in the Mark Index Entry dialog box, change the text in the Main Entry box to RAAF.**

5. **Select the Cross-Reference option and then click after** *See* **and type Royal Australian Air Force (see Figure 10-13).**

6. **Click the Mark button. Then close the dialog box.**

7. **Save the document and close it.**

Leave Word open for the next exercise.

Figure 10-13

Generating an index

After the document has been fully marked up for indexing, you can generate the index. Compared to marking, generating the index is fast and easy, requiring just a few steps.

In this exercise, you generate an index.

Files needed: Chapter 10 Bio Indexed.docx

1. **Open Chapter 10 Bio Indexed and save it as Chapter 10 Bio Final.**

2. **Move the insertion point to the end of the document, press Ctrl+Enter to start a new page, and choose References⇨Insert Index.**

   The Index dialog box opens.

3. **From the Formats drop-down list, choose Classic (see Figure 10-14) and then click OK.**

   The index appears in the document. See Figure 10-15.

Figure 10-14

4. **If nonprinting characters appear, choose Home⇨Show/Hide to hide all the index codes and other nonprinting characters.**

5. **Save and close the document.**

Leave Word open for the next exercise.

Figure 10-15

Captioning and Organizing Figures

In some documents, graphics are more than decoration. When graphics contribute to your document's content, you may want to number and caption each image. More to the point, you may want to use Word's tools for numbering and captioning each image automatically.

Automatically numbering your figure captions has a few benefits:

- You can reference the graphic by its number in your document to clarify how the graphic is connected to the text.

- If you move a graphic, Word automatically updates the caption numbering.

- Word can generate a Table of Figures, so it's easy to look up where a graphic appears in a document. A Table of Figures is like a Table of Contents, except a Table of Figures lists figures and captions based on their styles (instead of headings).

Attaching a caption to a figure

When you attach a caption to a figure, Word handles the task of keeping its numbering sequential. You can optionally add descriptive text to the caption if you like, or modify the numbering format.

In this exercise, you attach captions to figures.

Files needed: Chapter 10 Figures.docx

LINGO

A **caption** is a text label that describes a picture's content. Captions are usually numbered, such as Figure 1, to help describe which picture you're referring to.

1. **Open Chapter 10 Figures and save it as Chapter 10 Figures Captions.**

2. **Click the first graphic to select it and then choose References⇨Insert Caption.**

   The Caption dialog box opens. In the Caption box, the caption *Figure 1* already appears.

3. **Edit the caption to read** Figure 1: The Font group **(as shown in Figure 10-16) and then click OK.**

   The caption is added below the figure.

4. **Scroll down to the next page, click the second figure, and choose References⇨Insert Caption.**

   In the Caption box, Figure 2 already appears.

5. **Edit the caption to read** Figure 2: The Borders menu. **(See Figure 10-17.) Click OK.**

   The caption is added below the figure.

Figure 10-16

6. **Click the third figure in the document and then choose References⇨Insert Caption.**

7. **Change the** Figure 3 **caption to** Figure 3: The Alignment group **and then click OK.**

   The caption is added below the figure.

8. **Select the entire Text Formatting section of the document (from the Text Formatting heading through the figure caption below Figure 1), as shown in Figure 10-18.**

Figure 10-17

Select the text shown here.

Figure 10-18

9. **Press Ctrl+X to cut the selected text to the Clipboard; then click at the end of the document and press Ctrl+V to paste the Clipboard content.**

   The figure captions have not yet renumbered themselves.

10. **Press Ctrl+A to select the entire document and then press the F9 key to update the fields.**

The figure captions renumber according to their positions in the document.

To update an individual field code, you can also right-click the field code (the figure number, in this case) and choose Update Field on the shortcut menu.

11. **Save the document.**

Leave the document open for the next exercise.

If you want to make sure that the figure captions are always up to date when you print the document, choose File➪Options, and on the Display tab, select the Update Fields Before Printing check box.

Connecting text references to figure captions

In the preceding exercise, when you moved a section of the document and then updated the figure numbering, the references in-text to the figures did not update, so those references are now out of sync. For example, the paragraph before Figure 1 says, "as shown in Figure 2." You can solve this problem by using cross-references in the text instead of manually typing the numbers of the figures to which you refer.

LINGO

A **cross-reference** is an automatically updated reference to content elsewhere in the document.

In this exercise, you set up cross-references to figures.

Files needed: Chapter 10 Figures Captions.docx, open from the preceding exercise

1. **In the third paragraph of the Chapter 10 Figures Caption document, select the text *Figure 2* and then choose References➪Cross-Reference.**

The Cross-Reference dialog box opens.

2. From the Reference Type list, choose Figure; from the Insert Reference To list, choose Only Label and Number; from the For Which Caption list, choose Figure 1 (see Figure 10-19); and then click Insert.

3. Click Close to close the dialog box.

4. Scroll down to the next in-text figure reference (a reference to Figure 3 in the paragraph following the first figure), select the text *Figure 3,* and then choose References⇨Cross-Reference.

Figure 10-19

5. In the For Which Caption List, choose Figure 2: The Alignment group and then click Insert.

6. Leave the Cross-Reference dialog box open and drag it to the side so the document is visible.

7. Scroll down to the Text Formatting section of the document and select the text Figure 1; then in the Cross-Reference dialog box, select Figure 3: The Font group and click Insert.

8. Click Close to close the dialog box.

9. Save the document.

Leave the document open for the next exercise.

Creating a Table of Figures

A Table of Figures is not necessary in a short document, but in very long reports with dozens or hundreds of figures, it can help readers greatly by providing quick access to the numbered figures.

LINGO

A **Table of Figures** is like a Table of Contents except it lists the document's figures and their captions.

In this exercise, you create a Table of Figures.

Files needed: Chapter 10 Figures Captions.docx, open from the preceding exercise

1. **Click at the bottom of the Chapter 10 Figures Captions document to move the insertion point below the caption of the final figure and then press Ctrl+Enter to create a page break.**

2. **Type** Table of Figures, **and apply the Heading 1 style to the paragraph (from the Home tab, in the Styles group; see Figure 10-20).**

Figure 10-20

3. **Press Enter to start a new paragraph below the text you just typed and then choose References⇨Insert Table of Figures.**

   The Table of Figures dialog box opens.

4. **Deselect the Use Hyperlinks Instead of Page Numbers check box (see Figure 10-21) and then click OK to insert the Table of Figures.**

   The Table of Figures appears in the document, as shown in Figure 10-22.

Figure 10-21

Figure 10-22

5. Save the document and close it.

Leave Word open for the next exercise.

Organizing Legal Documents

Legal documents have some special requirements. For example, many legal documents use line numbering so that the parties reading them can easily refer to a specific line, and most legal documents include citations of court cases and other legal precedents. In the following sections, you learn how to use features in Word to accommodate those needs.

Turning on line numbering

Line numbering, if enabled, appears to the left of each line that contains text in your document. All lines are numbered except those in tables, footnotes, endnotes, text boxes, headers, and footers. You can choose to number every line individually or choose to display line numbers at intervals, such as every tenth line.

In this exercise, you create line numbering.

Files needed: Chapter 10 Contract.docx

1. **Open Chapter 10 Contract and save it as Chapter 10 Contract Numbers.**

2. **Choose Page Layout⇨Line Numbers⇨Continuous (see Figure 10-23).**

Blank lines created by pressing Enter are numbered along with other lines. However, blank lines created by applying extra spacing above or below a paragraph, or blank lines in between the lines of a double-spaced paragraph, are not numbered. Notice in Figure 10-23, for example, that lines 3 through 5 are blank numbered lines, and the extra line of spacing between lines 16 and 17 is not numbered.

Line numbers

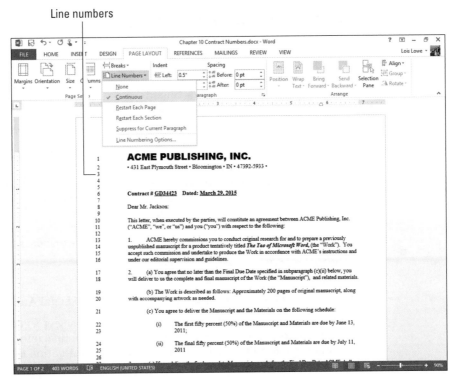

Figure 10-23

3. **Choose Page Layout⇨Line Numbers⇨Line Numbering Options.**

   The Page Setup dialog box opens with the Layout tab displayed.

4. **Click the Line Numbers button.**

   The Line Numbers dialog box opens.

5. **Change the Count By value to 10, as shown in Figure 10-24, click OK to close the Line Numbers dialog box, and then click OK to close the Page Setup dialog box.**

   The lines are now numbered every ten lines instead of every line.

6. **Save the document and close it.**

Leave Word open for the next exercise.

Figure 10-24

Creating a Table of Authorities

A Table of Authorities is common in a very long legal document to summarize the sources cited in the document. By creating a Table of Authorities, you provide an aid to other legal professionals who may work with the document and need to verify the sources cited.

LINGO

A **Table of Authorities** is like a Table of Contents except it refers only to citations of legal precedents (also known as **authorities**).

To create a Table of Authorities, you first enter each citation within the body of the document. Then you mark each one as a citation via Word's Mark Citation feature. Finally, you assemble the Table of Authorities, compiling all the marked citations.

In this exercise, you mark some legal citations and create a Table of Authorities.

Files needed: Chapter 10 Legal.docx

1. **Open Chapter 10 Legal and save it as Chapter 10 Legal Authorities.**

   Note: In this exercise, when you are instructed to select a citation, select all of the underlined citation text plus the parenthetical information that follows the underlined text. The parenthetical information is part of the citation.

2. **Select the first citation in the document and then choose References⇨Mark Citation.**

   The Mark Citation dialog box opens. See Figure 10-25.

3. **Click the Mark button.**

   A field code is inserted into the document.

4. **Click Close and examine the code that was inserted.**

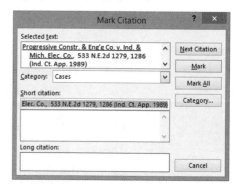

Figure 10-25

   The code is visible because Word switches to a view that includes hidden text and nonprinting characters when you open the Mark Citation dialog box. Figure 10-26 shows the inserted code for the first citation. The code is shaded in Figure 10-26 for easier readability but it won't appear shaded on your screen.

We·received·your·letter·of·March·15,·along·with·the·proposed·changes·to·the·Anderson·and·DeWitt·
contract.·-These·changes·would·be·unconscionable·and·are·therefore·Mr.·Anderson·and·Mr.·DeWitt·
decline·to·include·them.·-To·be·unconscionable,·a·contract·"must·be·such·as·no·sensible·man·not·under-
delusion,·duress·or·in·distress·would·make,·and·such·as·no·honest·and·fair·man·would·accept."·-
Progressive·Constr.·&·Eng'g·Co.·v.·Ind.·&·Mich.·Elec.·Co.,··533·N.E.2d·1279,·1286·(Ind.·Ct.·App.·1989)·TA-
\l·"Progressive·Constr.·&·Eng'g·Co.·v.·Ind.·&·Mich.·Elec.·Co.,··533·N.E.2d·1279,·1286·(Ind.·Ct.·App.·1989)"·
\s·"Progressive·Constr.·&·Eng'g·Co.·v.·Ind.·&·Mich.·Elec.·Co.,··533·N.E.2d·1279,·1286·(Ind.·Ct.·App.·1989)"·
\c·1.·-Federal·law·does·not·supplant·state·law·governing·the·unconscionability·of·adhesive·contracts.·-
Ingle·v.·Circuit·City·Stores,·Inc.,·328·F.3d·1165,·1169·(9th·Cir.·2003).¶

Figure 10-26

5. **Select the second citation in the document (the last line of the paragraph) and choose References⇨Mark Citation.**

   The Mark Citation dialog box opens, with the selected citation filled in. See Figure 10-27.

6. **Click the Mark button to mark the citation and then click Close to close the dialog box.**

7. **Choose Home⇨Show/Hide (see Figure 10-28) to toggle off the nonprinting characters (including the codes for the citations).**

Figure 10-27

Show/Hide button

Figure 10-28

8. **Click at the bottom of the document to move the insertion point there, press Ctrl+Enter to start a new page, type** Table of Authorities, **and apply the Heading 1 style to it.**

9. **Press Enter to start a new line and then choose References⇨Insert Table of Authorities. (It's in the Table of Authorities group.)**

The Table of Authorities dialog box opens. See Figure 10-29.

Figure 10-29

10. **Click OK to insert the Table of Authorities with the default settings.**

The Table of Authorities appears in the document. See Figure 10-30.

Table of Authorities

Cases

Ingle v. Circuit City Stores, Inc., 328 F.3d 1165, 1169 (9th Cir. 2003)...1
Progressive Constr. & Eng'g Co. v. Ind. & Mich. Elec. Co., 533 N.E.2d 1279, 1286 (Ind. Ct. App. 1989) 1

Figure 10-30

11. **Save the document and close it.**

Leave Word open for the next exercise.

Creating Footnotes and Endnotes

In Word, you can create either footnotes or endnotes in a variety of styles. Footnotes and endnotes can be used for bibliography information, such as citing the source of information or for explanatory information that may not be appropriate for inclusion in the body text.

Word's footnote and endnote tools help you create and place the note. These tools also keep the notes numbered sequentially and connect the superscript number in the text to the corresponding number next to each footnote or endnote.

Inserting a footnote

A footnote is an explanatory note that appears at the bottom of the same page where its reference number appears. When you use footnotes, the main part of the text stops a few lines earlier than normal on the page so there will be enough room for the footnote to appear. Word automatically adjusts the spacing for you to make the footnote appear in the right place.

Footnotes provide additional information that's not part of the main text. For example, a footnote could provide anecdotal information about a source you're citing. You can also use footnotes for source citations.

In this exercise, you create a footnote.

Files needed: Chapter 10 Williams.docx

1. **Open Chapter 10 Williams and save it as Chapter 10 Williams Bio.**

2. **Click at the end of the first sentence in the first paragraph under the Early Career heading to move the insertion point immediately after its period and then choose References⇨Insert Footnote.**

   A small number 1 appears at the spot where the insertion point was, and a corresponding footnote appears at the bottom of the page. The insertion point moves into the footnote, so you can type its text. See Figure 10-31.

Type the footnote here.

Figure 10-31

3. **Type** Garrison, Australian Dictionary of Biography, pp. 502–505.

4. **Select the text** *Australian Dictionary of Biography,* **and then choose Home⇨Italic (or press Ctrl+I) to italicize it.**

The footnote appears, as shown in Figure 10-32.

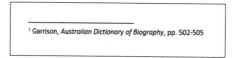

Figure 10-32

5. **Save the document.**

Leave the document open for the next exercise.

Inserting an endnote

Endnotes are useful when you need a notation system but don't want the notes to take up space at the bottom of each page. With endnotes, all the notes appear at the end of the document, in one list.

In this exercise, you create an endnote.

Files needed: Chapter 10 Williams Bio.docx, open from the preceding exercise

1. **In the Chapter 10 Williams Bio document, click at the end of the second sentence in the first paragraph under the heading Early Career to place the insertion point immediately after the period (see Figure 10-33).**

Place the insertion point here.

Early Career

Williams was born on 3 August 1890 into a working class family in Moonta Mines, South Australia.[1] He was the eldest son of Richard Williams, a copper miner who had emigrated from Cornwall, England, and his wife Emily. Leaving Moonta Public School at junior secondary level, Williams worked as a telegraph messenger and later as a bank clerk. He enlisted in a militia unit, the South Australian Infantry Regiment, in 1909 at the age of 19. Commissioned a second lieutenant in the 5th Australian Infantry Regiment on 5 March 1911, he joined the Permanent Military Forces the following year.

Figure 10-33

2. **Choose References⇨Insert Endnote.**

A small *i* (actually a lowercase Roman numeral) appears where the insertion point was. On the next page, below the last paragraph, an endnote section appears, and the insertion point moves into the note. See Figure 10-34.

How can you tell that the endnote section is not a footnote? Because it appears immediately following the last paragraph of the document, rather than appearing at the bottom of the page.

3. **Type** Odgers, The Royal Australian Air Force, p. 49.

Endnote marker. Notice that it can be
on a different page, unlike a footnote.

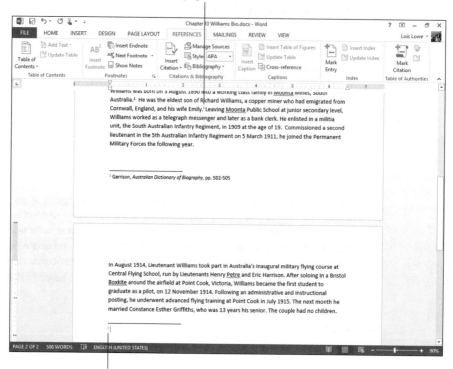

Type the endnote here.

Figure 10-34

4. **Select *The Royal Australian
Air Force,* and then choose
Home⇨Italic or press Ctrl+I to
italicize it.**

The endnote appears, as shown
in Figure 10-35.

> [1] Odgers, *The Royal Australian Air Force*, p. 49|

Figure 10-35

TIP

Word enables you to have both footnotes and endnotes in a document,
but that can get confusing for your readers. Experts recommend that you
stick with either footnotes or endnotes, one or the other, in a document.

5. **Save the document.**

Leave the document open for the next exercise.

Converting between footnotes and endnotes

Generally speaking, you should use one or the other in a document — footnotes or endnotes — but not both. Even though Word allows you to use both, as you did in the previous exercise, doing so can be confusing because the reader doesn't know where to look to find a note.

If you have used both footnotes and endnotes and now want to remedy that, or if you want to switch between using one or the other, Word makes it easy to do so.

In this exercise, you switch the endnotes in a document to footnotes.

Files needed: Chapter 10 Williams Bio. docx, open from the preceding exercise

Figure 10-36

1. **In the Chapter 10 Williams Bio document, on the References tab, click the dialog box launcher in the Footnotes group.**

   The Footnote and Endnote dialog box opens. See Figure 10-36.

2. **Click the Convert button.**

   The Convert Notes dialog box opens. See Figure 10-37.

3. **Select the Convert All Endnotes to Footnotes option and then click OK.**

   The endnote is converted to a footnote on page 1.

Figure 10-37

4. **Click Close to close the dialog box.**

5. **Save the document.**

Leave the document open for the next exercise.

Formatting footnotes and endnotes

You can change many aspects of footnotes and endnotes in your document, including what numbering scheme will be used for them, what the starting number will be, whether the numbering restarts on each page, and so on.

In this exercise, you change the numbering of footnotes to Roman, and then change them again to use symbols instead of numbers.

Files needed: Chapter 10 Williams Bio.docx, open from the preceding exercise

1. **In the Chapter 10 Williams Bio document, on the References tab, click the dialog box launcher in the Footnotes group.**

   The Footnote and Endnote dialog box opens.

2. **From the Number Format drop-down list, choose the uppercase Roman numerals (I, II, III), as shown in Figure 10-38, and then click Apply.**

   The new numbering format is applied in the document.

3. **On the References tab, click the dialog box launcher in the Footnotes group.**

   The Footnote and Endnote dialog box opens.

4. **From the Number Format drop-down list, choose the set of symbols at the bottom of the menu and then click Apply.**

   The symbols are applied as footnote markers.

5. **Save the document and close it.**

Exit Word.

Figure 10-38

Summing Up

In this chapter, you learned some techniques for organizing and formatting long documents. Here are the key points from this chapter:

- ✔ A Table of Contents provides a quick reference at the beginning of a document, including the major headings and their page numbers. To generate a TOC, choose References⇨Table of Contents.

- ✔ A TOC is based on styles, so before generating your TOC, make sure your headings are formatted using heading styles.

- ✔ To update a TOC, choose References⇨Update Table.

- ✔ To create an index, first mark the words to be made into entries by choosing References⇨Mark Entry. Then generate the index by choosing References⇨Insert Index.

- ✔ Word's figure captioning feature auto-numbers figures sequentially in the document and enables you to generate a Table of Figures. To add a figure caption, choose References⇨Insert Caption.

- ✔ To create a cross-reference, choose References⇨Cross-Reference.

- ✔ To create a Table of Figures, choose References⇨Insert Table of Figures.

- ✔ Legal documents often require line numbering. To number lines, choose Page Layout⇨Line Numbers⇨Continuous.

- ✔ A Table of Authorities is a summary of legal citations in a document. To create one, first mark the citations by choosing References⇨Mark Citation. Then choose References⇨Insert Table of Authorities to generate the table.

- ✔ To add a footnote, choose References⇨Insert Footnote. To add an endnote, choose References⇨Insert Endnote.

Try-it-yourself lab

For more practice with the features covered in this chapter, try the following exercise on your own:

1. **Open a multipage document that you've created and save it as Chapter 10 Try It.**

   If you don't already have a multipage document, copy some text from a book from Project Gutenberg (www.gutenberg.org), an archive of books that are no longer copyrighted.

2. **Add a Table of Contents, an index, and at least one footnote or end-note to the document.**

3. **Save all changes if prompted and exit Word.**

Know this tech talk

caption: A text label that describes a piece of artwork.

cross-reference: A reference to another location elsewhere in a document.

endnote: An explanatory note that appears at the end of a document.

footnote: An explanatory note that appears at the bottom of a page.

index: An alphabetical listing of important terms and the page numbers on which they appear.

Table of Authorities: A Table of Contents that refers to citations of legal precedents.

Table of Contents: An ordered list of the headings or other major elements in a document.

Table of Figures: A listing of the figures in a document.

Chapter 11

Protecting and Sharing a Document

✔ Turning on change tracking enables you to *see what you and other people have changed in a document.*

✔ Accepting or rejecting revisions *gives you control over the changes* that others make.

✔ Comments *enable multiple reviewers to communicate* with each other.

✔ The Compatibility Checker helps *determine whether people with earlier versions of Word can see your document* the way you intended.

This chapter covers many of Word's most popular features for managing the process of sharing your work with others. Word makes it easy to track the changes and comments made by multiple users, and then integrate them into a combined final version that takes everyone's changes into account.

Word can also remove certain features of a document to make it more compatible with earlier versions of Word — which can be very useful if some of the people on your editing team don't use the latest Office release.

Tracking Document Changes

Word can track many types of document changes, including insertions, deletions, moves, and formatting modifications. In the following sections, you learn how to enable and configure how edits to a document are tracked and how revision marks appear onscreen. You also learn how to accept or reject revisions.

Turning on change tracking

By default, change tracking is turned off. When you turn it on, Word begins noting each change you make, using a standard set of marks, such as underlining for insertions and strikethrough for deletions.

In this exercise, you enable change tracking in a document.

Files needed: Chapter 11 Bio.docx

1. **Open Chapter 11 Bio, save it as Chapter 11 Bio Revisions, and then choose Review⇨Track Changes.**

   The Track Changes button becomes highlighted. See Figure 11-1.

Track Changes button

Figure 11-1

2. **On the Review tab, open the Display for Review drop-down list and choose All Markup.**

   New in Word 2013 is the ability to show all markup or just certain types. For now, choose to see all the revisions.

3. **In the first paragraph, delete *British* and type** United Kingdom **in its place.**

   British turns red and appears in strikethrough, and *United Kingdom* appears underlined.

4. **On the first line of the first body paragraph, select *Sir Richard Williams* and press Ctrl+B to make it bold.**

   A balloon appears to the right of the paragraph showing the formatting change. See Figure 11-2.

Boldface the name.   This balloon shows the formatting change.

Richard Williams

Air Marshal **Sir Richard Williams** KBE, CB, DSO (3 August 1890 – 7 February 1980) is widely regarded as the "father" of the Royal Australian Air Force (RAAF). He was the first military pilot trained in Australia, and went on to command Australian and ~~British~~ United Kingdom fighter units in World War I. A proponent for air power independent of other branches of the armed services, Williams played a leading role in the establishment of the RAAF and became its first Chief of the Air Staff (CAS) in 1922. He served as CAS for thirteen years over three terms, longer than any other officer.

Lois Lowe
Formatted: Font: Bold

Figure 11-2

5. **Save the document.**

Leave the document open for the next exercise.

Customizing the display of markup

You can control how much markup you see onscreen. Sometimes it may be appropriate to see every little change, down to the last comma, whereas other times a big-picture approach is better.

In this exercise, you set certain types of changes to display or hide.

Files needed: Chapter 11 Bio Revisions.docx, open from the preceding exercise

1. **Choose Review➪Display for Review and select Simple Markup.**

   See Figure 11-3. Note that the markings from the previous exercise are no longer shown. Along the left side of the paragraph are two short red lines indicating which lines of the paragraph contain changes.

2. **Choose Review➪Display for Review and select All Markup.**

   All revisions are shown.

Red lines indicate lines
where changes were made.

Markup does not appear.

Choose Simple Markup.

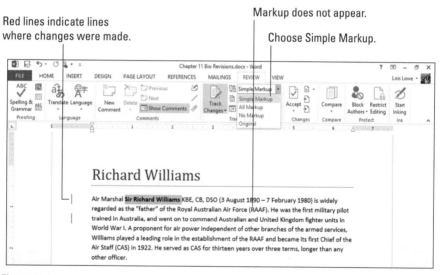

Figure 11-3

3. **Choose Review⇨Show Markup, and on the menu that appears, note the types of markup that you can display or hide.**

See Figure 11-4. For example, you can choose to include or exclude Comments, Ink, Insertions and Deletions, and Formatting. You can also choose to see comments from only specific people.

Figure 11-4

4. **Click Formatting to deselect formatting from the list of markup types shown.**

The balloon showing the bold formatting change disappears.

5. **Click the dialog box launcher in the Tracking group.**

The Track Changes Options dialog box opens. See Figure 11-5. This dialog box contains many of the same options that you find on the Show Markup menu (which you open in Step 3). The dialog box holds a few additional items, too.

6. **Click the Advanced Options button.**

The Advanced Track Changes Options dialog box opens. See Figure 11-6.

Figure 11-5

Figure 11-6

7. Take note of the various colors and symbols that are set to mark the different types of changes.

For example, note that the color of insertions and deletions depends on the author (with a different color assigned to each author).

8. Click the Cancel button to close the Advanced Track Changes Options dialog box without making any changes. Then click Cancel (or Close) to close the Track Changes Options dialog box without making any changes.

9. Choose Review⇨Show Markup⇨Ink to deselect the Ink option.

The Ink feature, available in most Office applications, enables users to annotate a document by drawing on it using a finger or stylus (on a touchscreen) or by dragging with the mouse. Most people don't use it, so it's a good type of change-tracking to turn off as practice for customizing your change-tracking settings.

10. Choose Review⇨Show Markup⇨Balloons⇨Show Revisions in Balloons.

See Figure 11-7. The deletion of *British* now appears in a balloon. The addition of *United Kingdom* doesn't appear in a balloon because it's an insertion.

Choose whether revisions appear in balloons.

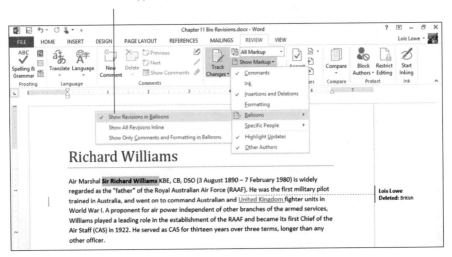

Figure 11-7

11. Choose Review⇨Show Markup⇨Balloons⇨Show All Revisions Inline.

The markup area disappears from the right side of the document and all balloons disappear.

12. From the Display for Review drop-down list, choose No Markup.

All revisions are shown, but all revision marks are hidden.

13. From the Display for Review drop-down list, choose Original.

All revisions are hidden, and all review marks are also hidden.

14. From the Display for Review drop-down list, choose All Markup.

All revisions are displayed, and all review marks are also displayed.

15. Choose Review⇨Reviewing Pane (click the arrow, not the button face)⇨Reviewing Pane Vertical.

A Revisions pane appears to the left of the document, showing each revision. See Figure 11-8.

Revisions pane

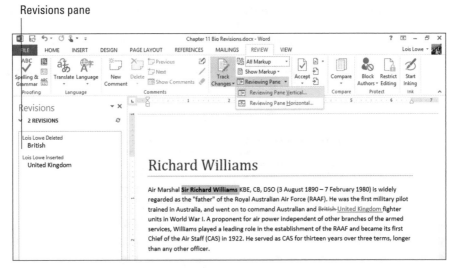

Figure 11-8

16. **Choose Review⇨Reviewing Pane⇨Reviewing Pane Horizontal.**

    The task pane moves to the bottom of the document.

17. **Choose Review⇨Reviewing Pane (click the button face, not the arrow).**

    The Reviewing pane disappears.

18. **Save the document.**

Leave the document open for the next exercise.

Accepting or rejecting a revision

When you accept a revision, the change is incorporated into the document and the revision mark goes away. When you reject a revision, the change is discarded and the revision mark goes away. You can accept or reject each revision individually, or you can accept or reject all revisions in the entire document at once.

In this exercise, you make some revisions, and then accept or reject them.

Files needed: Chapter 11 Bio Revisions.docx, open from the preceding exercise

1. **In the Chapter 11 Bio Revisions document, in the first body paragraph, delete *thirteen* and type** 13 **to replace it.**

   The change appears with revision marks. See Figure 11-9.

   > Air Marshal **Sir Richard Williams** KBE, CB, DSO (3 August 1890 – 7 February 1980) is widely regarded as the "father" of the Royal Australian Air Force (RAAF). He was the first military pilot trained in Australia, and went on to command Australian and ~~British~~ United Kingdom fighter units in World War I. A proponent for air power independent of other branches of the armed services, Williams played a leading role in the establishment of the RAAF and became its first Chief of the Air Staff (CAS) in 1922. He served as CAS for ~~thirteen~~ 13 years over three terms, longer than any other officer.

   Figure 11-9

2. **Click at the beginning of the first paragraph to move the insertion point there; then choose Review⇨Next Change, found in the Changes group, to move the insertion point to the first change (the deletion of *British*).**

3. **Choose Review⇨Accept to accept that change.**

   The next change is highlighted (the insertion of *United Kingdom*).

4. **Click Accept.**

   The next change is highlighted (the deletion of *thirteen*).

5. **Click Accept.**

   The next change is highlighted (the insertion of *13*).

6. **Click Accept.**

   The next change is highlighted (the bold formatting applied to *Sir Richard Williams*).

7. **Click Reject.**

   A dialog box appears telling you that there are no more changes. See Figure 11-10.

   Figure 11-10

8. Click OK.

The dialog box closes and the paragraph appears, as shown in Figure 11-11.

Air Marshal Sir Richard Williams KBE, CB, DSO (3 August 1890 – 7 February 1980) is widely regarded as the "father" of the Royal Australian Air Force (RAAF). He was the first military pilot trained in Australia, and went on to command Australian and United Kingdom fighter units in World War I. A proponent for air power independent of other branches of the armed services, Williams played a leading role in the establishment of the RAAF and became its first Chief of the Air Staff (CAS) in 1922. He served as CAS for 13 years over three terms, longer than any other officer.

Figure 11-11

9. Save the document.

Leave the document open for the next exercise.

Accepting or rejecting all revisions

If you're confident about the revisions, you might want to accept them all at once. For example, if you made them all yourself, you might already know that they're all valid changes. Conversely, if you want to discard all the changes at once (for example, if someone heavily edited a document and you preferred it the original way), you can do that as well.

In this exercise, you make some revisions and then reject them all.

Files needed: Chapter 11 Bio Revisions.docx, open from the preceding exercise

1. In the Chapter 11 Bio Revisions document, in the first body paragraph, in the first line, delete *1980* and type 1982; in the second body paragraph, delete *1914* and type 1915; and in the second body paragraph, capitalize Lieutenant Colonel. Figure 11-12 shows the second body paragraph with the revisions made.

Williams came from a working class background in South Australia. He was a lieutenant in the Army when he learned to fly at Point Cook, Victoria, in 19141915. As a pilot with the Australian Flying Corps (AFC) in World War I, Williams rose to command No. 1 Squadron AFC, and later 40th Wing RAF. He was awarded the Distinguished Service Order and finished the war a Lieutenant Colonel. Afterwards he campaigned for an Australian Air Force run separately to the Army and Navy, which came into being on 31 March 1921.

Figure 11-12

2. **On the Review tab, click the arrow button next to the Reject and Move to Next button in the Changes group, and click Reject All Changes on the menu that appears. See Figure 11-13.**

   All the changes you made are reversed, and the revision marks disappear.

3. **Save the document.**

Leave the document open for the next exercise.

Reject and Move to Next button

Figure 11-13

Preventing untracked changes

If you're using the Track Changes feature in Word to ensure that nobody makes any unnoticed changes in a document, you may want to take a further security step and restrict changes to tracked ones only. You can also password-protect this restriction so that nobody can sneak changes into your document without them being tracked.

In this exercise, you prevent a document from being changed without change tracking.

Files needed: Chapter 11 Bio Revisions.docx, open from the preceding exercise

1. **In the Chapter 11 Bio Revisions document, choose Review⇨Restrict Editing.**

   The Restrict Editing task pane opens to the right of the document. See Figure 11-14.

2. **In the Editing Restrictions section, select the Allow Only This Type of Editing in the Document check box, choose Tracked Changes from the drop-down list, and then click the Yes, Start Enforcing Protection button.**

   The Start Enforcing Protection dialog box opens.

3. **In the Start Enforcing Protection box, click OK (see Figure 11-15).**

Figure 11-14

You can password-protect change tracking, but in this exercise, you don't.

You can leave the
password fields blank
for this exercise.

Figure 11-15

4. **Try to choose Review⇨Track Changes.**

   The Track Changes button is disabled, so nothing happens.

5. **In the Restrict Editing task pane, click the Stop Protection button.**

   The Track Changes button is once again clickable.

6. **Choose Review⇨Restrict Editing to close the task pane.**

7. **Save the document.**

Leave the document open for the next exercise.

Working with Document Comments

Comments enable users to write notes to each other within the document. You might create a comment to express an opinion about someone else's edit of a particular sentence, for example, or to explain the reasoning behind your edit. Then when you're ready to review the comments in the document, you can use the Review tab to easily move between comments.

LINGO

Comments are nonprinting notes you can attach to certain parts of a document to exchange information with other contributors.

In the following exercises, you learn how to insert, review, and delete comments.

Inserting a comment

Comments appear, by default, in balloons to the right of the document, like some revisions do. They also appear in the Reviewing pane, if displayed. When multiple users add comments to a document, each person's comments appear in a different color balloon (or bar in the Reviewing pane, if balloons are disabled). If a user makes revisions and adds comments to the document, their revision marks and comment balloons are the same color.

In this exercise, you insert comments in a document.

Files needed: Chapter 11 Bio Revisions.docx, open from the preceding exercise

1. **In the Chapter 11 Bio Revisions document, in the first paragraph, select *February 1980* and then choose Review⇨New Comment.**

   The Reviewing pane appears below the document (because that's the last location you specified for it). Balloons don't appear for comments because you turned off that feature in an earlier exercise. The insertion point moves to the comment.

2. **Type** Is this accurate?.

   The text you type appears in the Reviewing pane, under the Comment heading. See Figure 11-16.

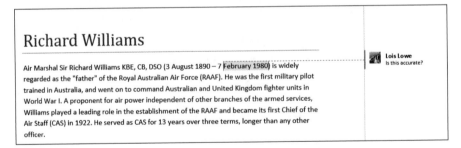

Figure 11-16

3. **On the Review tab, click the dialog box launcher in the Tracking group.**

   The Track Changes Options dialog box opens.

4. **From the Balloons in All Markup View Show drop-down list, choose Comments and Formatting (see Figure 11-17) and then click OK.**

   The comment appears in a balloon to the right of the document.

Figure 11-17

5. Choose Review⇨Reviewing Pane (the button face, not the arrow) to turn off the Reviewing pane.

The Reviewing pane is no longer needed because the comments already appear. Figure 11-18 shows the comment in a balloon.

New Comment button

Toggle the Revisions pane on and off.

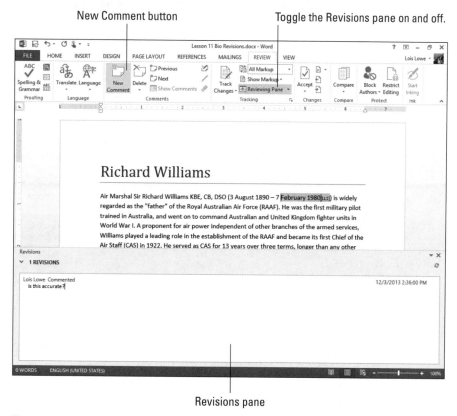

Revisions pane

Figure 11-18

6. Scroll to the bottom of the document, select *Constance Esther Griffiths* and then choose Review⇨New Comment.

A new comment balloon appears.

7. Type Verify middle name and then press Ctrl+Home to return to the top of the document.

8. Save the document.

Leave the document open for the next exercise.

Reviewing comments

In a short document, you can easily scroll through and examine the comments, especially if they're in balloons. In a very long document, however, you may find it easier to use the Next and Previous buttons on the Review tab's Comments group to move from one comment to another.

In this exercise, you review the comments in a document.

Files needed: Chapter 11 Bio Revisions.docx, open from the preceding exercise

1. **In the Chapter 11 Bio Revisions document, choose Review⇨Next Comment, found in the Comments group.**

   Make sure you click the Next Comment button in the Comments group, not the Next Change button in the Changes group. The first comment becomes selected. See Figure 11-19.

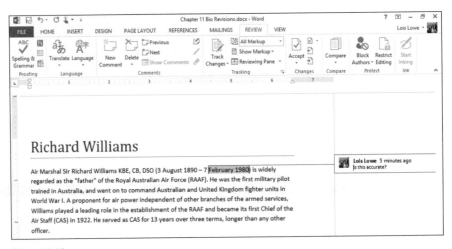

Figure 11-19

2. **Click Next Comment again.**

   The next comment appears.

3. **Click Previous Comment.**

   The previous comment appears.

4. **Press Ctrl+Home to return to the beginning of the document.**

Leave the document open for the next exercise.

Deleting a comment

After you review a comment, you may want to delete it.

To choose whether to include comments when printing, choose File⇨Print and then click the Print All Pages button. At the bottom of the menu that appears is a Print Markup command. If this command is selected, comments will print; if it isn't, they won't. Click the command to toggle its setting.

In this exercise, you delete comments from a document.

Files needed: Chapter 11 Bio Revisions.docx, open from the preceding exercise

1. **In the Chapter 11 Bio Revisions document, choose Review⇨Next Comment, found in the Comments section, to move to the first comment.**

2. **In the Comments group, click Delete to delete the comment.**

3. **Click Next Comment again to go to the next comment.**

4. **In the Comments group, click the down arrow next to the Delete button and then click Delete All Comments in Document to remove all remaining comments from the document (see Figure 11-20).**

Click the arrow to open the menu.

Figure 11-20

5. **Save the document.**

Leave the document open for the next exercise.

Marking a Document as Final

After accepting the edits in your document, you may want to discourage other people from making additional changes to it. One way to do this is to use the Mark as Final feature in Word to temporarily disable editing for that document.

Marking a document as final is not a security measure because anyone can easily override it; however, it does make the user stop and think before making an edit.

In this exercise, you mark a document as final, and then override that setting.

Files needed: Chapter 11 Bio Revisions.docx, open from the preceding exercise

1. **In the Chapter 11 Bio Revisions document, choose File⟹Info⟹Protect Document⟹Mark as Final (see Figure 11-21).**

   A message appears that the document will be marked as final and then saved.

Figure 11-21

2. **Click OK.**

A message appears that the document has been marked as final (see Figure 11-22).

Figure 11-22

3. **Click OK.**

4. **Press Esc or click the Back arrow button to exit Backstage view.**

An information bar appears across the top of the document, and the Ribbon doesn't appear except for its tab names. See Figure 11-23.

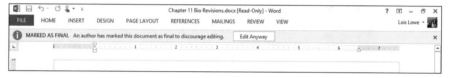

Figure 11-23

5. **Click the Edit Anyway button.**

The Ribbon returns, and the document is no longer marked as final.

6. **Save and close the document.**

Leave Word open for the next exercise.

Using the Compatibility Checker

If you want to share your work with someone who uses an earlier version of Word, you may have some compatibility issues. The Compatibility Checker enables you to check whether a document will share without any problems. For each incompatibility, the Compatibility Checker explains what will be done to resolve the problem, but it doesn't make any changes to your document.

In this exercise, you run the Compatibility Checker for a document.

Files needed: Chapter 11 Compatibility.docx

1. **Open Chapter 11 Compatibility and save it as Chapter 11 Compatibility Checked.**

2. **Choose File⇨Info⇨Check for Issues⇨Check Compatibility (see Figure 11-24).**

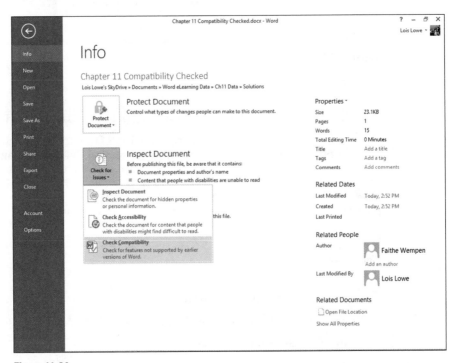

Figure 11-24

The Microsoft Word Compatibility Checker dialog box opens, as shown in Figure 11-25. The wording in the dialog box might be slightly different than shown here if the file is saved in a remote location, such as on your SkyDrive.

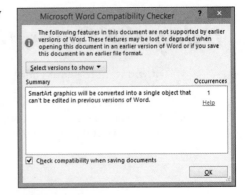

Figure 11-25

3. **Click the Help hyperlink.**

   The Word Help window opens, displaying an article that describes the compatibility issues that it looks for.

4. **Read the article and then close the Word Help window.**

5. **Click OK to close the dialog box.**

6. **Save the document and close it.**

Exit Word.

 Summing Up

This chapter covers methods of managing documents that have multiple contributors. Here are the key points from this chapter:

- To track changes in the document, choose Review⇨Track Changes. You can use the Track Changes Options dialog box to fine-tune what is tracked and how it's tracked. Use the dialog box launcher in the Tracking group to open it.

- To display or hide various types of change markup, choose Review⇨Show Markup.

- You can accept or reject each change in a document. Use the Accept and Reject buttons in the Changes group for individual edits. You can also accept or reject all remaining changes by using the commands on those buttons' drop-down lists.

- You can prevent others from making untracked changes by choosing Review⇨Restrict Editing.

- Comments enable contributors to leave messages for one another that aren't part of the main document. To insert a comment, choose Review⇨New Comment. To review comments in a document, choose Review⇨Next Comment, in the Comments group.

- Marking a document as final disables editing for the document; it isn't a security feature because it can be overridden easily. To mark a document as final, choose File⇨Info⇨Protect Document⇨Mark as Final.

- The Compatibility Checker checks a document to make sure people with earlier versions of Word can read it. Choose File⇨Info⇨Check for Issues⇨Check Compatibility.

Try-it-yourself lab

For more practice with the features covered in this chapter, try the following exercise on your own:

1. Write a memo proposing a change to a policy at your workplace or school and save it as Chapter 11 Memo.

2. Add comments to the document and then turn on revision marks.

3. Send the document to a friend, and ask him to make at least one revision to it and send it back to you.

4. Review the changes, and then accept or reject them.

5. Review and delete the comments and then mark the document as final.

6. Close the document and exit Word.

Know this tech talk

comment: A note inserted in a document, usually containing a question or explanation of a part of the document.

Mark as Final: To make a file uneditable, preventing accidental changes to it. The read-only aspect can be overridden easily.

Appendix
Essential SkyDrive Skills

SkyDrive is a Microsoft-owned cloud-based storage space. Each user has his or her own storage area for storing private files, sharing files with specific others, or making files publicly available. A certain amount of storage space is free, and you can pay if you want more than what's provided. (The amount of storage space available depends on when you signed up for your account and what type of account you have.)

As you see in your work with Word throughout this eLearning kit, your SkyDrive is your default save location for Word and other Office apps. Using SkyDrive as your main document storage area has several consequences:

- ✔ You can access your files from any computer, whether or not Word is installed on that computer.
- ✔ You can share your work with other people without sending them separate copies of a file or files.
- ✔ Your files are available only when Internet access is available (hence the term *cloud storage, cloud* being a term used to describe services hosted online).

You can get around that last drawback by installing the SkyDrive for Windows app on your PC, which automatically mirrors the content of your SkyDrive on your PC and keeps the copy in sync with the SkyDrive's actual content.

There are several ways of accessing your SkyDrive. This appendix covers the four major ways:

- ✔ Access your SkyDrive space on the web via `www.skydrive.com`.
- ✔ Use the SkyDrive for Windows desktop app.
- ✔ Use the Windows 8 SkyDrive app on a PC or tablet that has Windows 8 installed.
- ✔ Use the SkyDrive links within Word when saving or opening files.

Note that, as I write this appendix, Microsoft's cloud storage is named SkyDrive, but Microsoft is preparing to rename the service OneDrive. For the purposes of this appendix, know that when I say SkyDrive, I'm referring to Microsoft's cloud storage.

Understanding Your SkyDrive Interface Options

There are several ways to access your SkyDrive; each of the following sections explains one of the methods.

Signing into the SkyDrive web interface

Some SkyDrive management activities can only be performed via the SkyDrive web interface, so you should know how to access it. To get started, point your browser to www.skydrive.com. (The page will redirect to the server where Microsoft is hosting SkyDrive at the moment. As of this writing, it is https://skydrive.live.com but by the time you read this, it may have changed.)

If you already have a Microsoft account and your computer is set up to automatically sign you into it, your SkyDrive's content appears automatically. From the SkyDrive web interface, you can click folders and files to open them, or use the buttons on the toolbar at the top of the window to perform other actions. I tell you more about those actions later in this appendix.

Installing and using SkyDrive for Windows desktop

If you want to access your SkyDrive files offline and make managing SkyDrive files as easy as managing your local files, install the SkyDrive for Windows app on your PC.

The SkyDrive for Windows app automatically mirrors the content of your SkyDrive on your PC and keeps the copy in sync with the SkyDrive's actual content. If you are ever not connected to the Internet, it allows you to work on local copies of your files, and then it automatically uploads the updates to your SkyDrive the next time Internet connectivity is available. The SkyDrive for Windows app also places a shortcut to your locally mirrored copies of your SkyDrive content on the Favorites list in File Explorer (or Windows Explorer), so you can easily access them with one click.

To get SkyDrive for Windows, open the SkyDrive web interface, as described in the preceding section, and then in the navigation pane at the left, click the Get SkyDrive Apps hyperlink. From there, find and follow the link for the Windows desktop apps. Click Download Now and follow the prompts to complete the installation. (I'm being intentionally vague about the steps here because by the time you read this, they may have changed; Microsoft updates its websites frequently.)

After you install SkyDrive for Windows, you see a SkyDrive shortcut in the Favorites list in File Explorer (Windows 8) or Windows Explorer (Windows 7). This shortcut points to a folder on your hard drive: `C:\Users\username\SkyDrive`. This folder is a staging area for your online SkyDrive and is automatically synchronized with it. The green check mark on each icon indicates that it has been synchronized. In other words, the copies on SkyDrive are identical to these copies on your local machine. When the copies are out of sync because an update hasn't occurred yet, a pair of blue arrows appears on the icon to indicate a sync is scheduled or in process. If there is a problem with a sync (such as Internet unavailability), a red x symbol appears on the icon to indicate that.

Managing SkyDrive files within Word

You can save and open files on your SkyDrive from within Word. When you choose Save As from the File menu, the default save location is your SkyDrive. You can click Browse to browse your SkyDrive's content, or you can click one of the folder names under Recent Folders to access one of the folders within your SkyDrive.

Using the Windows 8 SkyDrive app

If you are running Windows 8, you can access the Windows 8 SkyDrive app from the Start screen. It's a tablet-style app optimized for touchscreens, like the other new Windows 8 applications. Access the SkyDrive app from its tile on the Start screen.

Within the SkyDrive app, you see your folders listed to the left, with picture previews of the folders' content if available. To the right of the folders, you'll see tiles for any files that are stored at the top level of your SkyDrive's organizational system, not in any particular folder. Right-click to open a command bar at the bottom of the screen. From this bar, you can choose commands to work with your content. Using the commands on the command bar, you can do all the basic file management tasks from the Windows 8 SkyDrive app, such as uploading and downloading, creating new folders, deleting, renaming, and moving. (Those latter three commands are on a submenu when you choose Manage.)

When you click a file or folder, it opens. If it's a file, it opens in its default program. To choose some other program in which to open the file, click Open With on the command bar and then select the desired app from the menu that appears.

Managing Files on Your SkyDrive

In the following sections, you learn how to perform basic file management activities on your SkyDrive, including uploading and downloading, copying, moving, deleting, and renaming files.

Uploading a file

Uploading means transferring a file from your local hard drive, or some other local location, to your SkyDrive. The procedure for placing a file on your SkyDrive depends on which interface you are using. Table A-1 summarizes the steps by interface type.

Table A-1	Uploading to Your SkyDrive
Interface Type	*Steps*
Web interface	1. Display the folder in which you want to place the file.
	2. Click the Upload button in the toolbar.
	3. Select the file to upload.
	4. Click Open.
SkyDrive for Windows	1. In File Explorer (Windows Explorer), select the file.
	2. Press Ctrl+C to copy the file to the Clipboard.
	3. In the Favorites bar, click SkyDrive.
	4. Navigate to the desired folder on your SkyDrive.
	5. Press Ctrl+V to paste the file.
Word 2013	1. Choose File➪Save As.
	2. Click Browse.
	3. Navigate to the desired folder on your SkyDrive.
	4. Type a filename in the File name box.
	5. Click OK.

Interface Type	Steps
Windows 8 SkyDrive app	1. Display the folder in which you want to place the file.
	2. Right-click to display command bar.
	3. Click Upload.
	4. Select the file to upload.
	5. Click Add to SkyDrive.

Downloading a file from your SkyDrive

Downloading means copying a file from your SkyDrive to a local drive, such as your hard drive. Table A-2 summarizes the steps by interface type.

Table A-2	Downloading from Your SkyDrive
Interface Type	*Steps*
Web interface	1. Click the check mark next to a file's name to select it.
	2. Click the Download button in the toolbar.
	3. If prompted by your browser to open or save, click Save.
	4. If prompted for a save location, choose it and click Save. (Some browsers do not prompt for a save location; they save all downloads to a default location.)
SkyDrive for Windows	1. In File Explorer (Windows Explorer), click SkyDrive in the Favorites list.
	2. Select the file to be downloaded.
	3. Press Ctrl+C to copy the file to the Clipboard.
	4. Navigate to a local folder location.
	5. Press Ctrl+V to paste the file.

continued

Table A-2 *(continued)*

Interface Type	Steps
Word 2013	1. Choose File⇨Open.
	2. Click Browse.
	3. Select the file on your SkyDrive.
	4. Click Open.
	5. Choose File⇨Save As.
	6. Click Computer and then click Browse.
	7. Navigate to a local folder location.
	8. Click OK.
Windows 8 SkyDrive app	1. Right-click the file to select it.
	2. Click Download.
	3. Navigate to a local folder location.
	4. Click Choose This Folder.
	5. Click OK.

Renaming a file or folder

One way to rename a file is to save it with a different name and then delete the original. However, it's much easier to directly rename a file with the Rename command. Table A-3 summarizes the steps for renaming a file or folder on your SkyDrive.

Table A-3	Renaming a File or Folder on Your SkyDrive
Interface Type	**Steps**
Web interface	1. Click the check mark next to a file's name to select it.
	2. Click the Manage button on the toolbar.
	3. Click Rename.
	4. Type the new name and press Enter.

Interface Type	Steps
SkyDrive for Windows	1. In File Explorer (Windows Explorer), click the file you want to rename.
	2. Click Home⇨Rename.
	3. Type the new name and press Enter.
Word 2013	1. Choose File⇨Open.
	2. Click Browse.
	3. Right-click the file on your SkyDrive.
	4. Choose Rename.
	5. Type the new name and press Enter.
Windows 8 SkyDrive app	1. Right-click the file to select it.
	2. Click Manage.
	3. Click Rename.
	4. Type the new name and press Enter.

Moving or copying a file or folder

Moving and copying, in the context of this section, refer to moving or copying within the SkyDrive itself, from one folder to another, and not into or out of the SkyDrive (which would be considered uploading or downloading, respectively, and which were covered earlier in this appendix). Table A-4 explains how to move and copy files or folders on your SkyDrive.

Table A-4   Moving or Copying a File or Folder on Your SkyDrive

Interface Type	Moving	Copying
Web interface	1. Click the check mark next to a file or folder's name to select it.	1. Click the check mark next to a file or folder's name to select it.
	2. Click the Manage button on the toolbar.	2. Click the Manage button on the toolbar.
	3. Click Move to.	3. Click Copy To.
	4. Click the desired folder in the dialog box.	4. Click the desired folder in the dialog box.
	5. Click Move.	5. Click Copy.

continued

Table A-4 *(continued)*

Interface Type	Moving	Copying
SkyDrive for Windows	1. In File Explorer (Windows Explorer), click the file or folder you want to move. 2. Press Ctrl+X or choose Home⇨Cut. 3. Navigate to the folder where you want to move the file or folder. 4. Press Ctrl+V or choose Home⇨Paste.	1. In File Explorer (Windows Explorer), click the file or folder you want to move. 2. Press Ctrl+C or choose Home⇨Copy. 3. Navigate to the folder where you want to copy the file or folder. 4. Press Ctrl+V or choose Home⇨Paste.
Word 2013	1. Choose File⇨Open. 2. Click Browse. 3. Right-click the file or folder on your SkyDrive and click Cut, or press Ctrl+X. 4. Navigate to the folder where you want to move the file or folder. 5. Right-click an empty area and choose Paste, or press Ctrl+V.	1. Choose File⇨Open. 2. Click Browse. 3. Right-click the file or folder on your SkyDrive and click Copy, or press Ctrl+C. 4. Navigate to the folder where you want to move the file or folder. 5. Right-click an empty area and choose Paste, or press Ctrl+V.
Windows 8 SkyDrive app	1. Right-click the file or folder to select it. 2. Click Manage. 3. Click Move. 4. Navigate to the folder where you want to move the file or folder. 5. Click Move Here.	Not applicable; you can't copy files or folders in this app.

Deleting a file or folder

Deleting a file or folder removes it. A Recycle Bin is available for retrieving deleted files on your SkyDrive, but it is accessible only from the web interface.

Table A-5 summarizes the steps for deleting files and folders on your SkyDrive.

Table A-5	Deleting a File or Folder on Your SkyDrive	
Interface Type	*Deleting*	*Restoring a Deleted File*
Web interface	1. Click the check mark next to a file or folder's name to select it. 2. Click the Manage button. 3. Click Delete.	1. Click Recycle Bin at the bottom of the navigation pane at the left. 2. Click the check mark next to a file or folder's name to select it. 3. Click Restore.
SkyDrive for Windows	1. In File Explorer (Windows Explorer), click the file or folder you want to delete. 2. Press the Delete key, or choose Home⇨Delete.	1. Open the Recycle Bin from your Windows desktop. 2. Click the file to restore. 3. Click Restore the Selected Items.
Word 2013	1. Choose File⇨Open. 2. Click Browse. 3. Click the file or folder on your SkyDrive. 4. Press the Delete key.	To immediately restore a deletion, press Ctrl+Z. Otherwise, use the web interface or SkyDrive for Windows to restore the file.
Windows 8 SkyDrive app	1. Right-click the file or folder to select it. 2. Click Manage. 3. Click Delete. 4. Click Delete to confirm. 5. Click Move Here.	Not applicable; you can't restore files or folders in this app.

314
Appendix: Essential SkyDrive Skills

Sharing SkyDrive files with others

SkyDrive offers a variety of ways to share your SkyDrive files with other people. You can send e-mail, post a link to Facebook, or create a hyperlink that you can then share with others any way you like (such as pasting it into the HTML for a web page or pasting it into an instant message program).

Sharing is configured primarily through the web interface; the other interfaces aren't designed for doing it. However, in some cases you can access a command in another interface that will automatically open the web interface and start the sharing process. Table A-6 summarizes the methods of sharing.

Table A-6	Sharing a File on Your SkyDrive	
Interface Type	*Sharing via E-Mail*	*Getting a Share Link*
Web interface	1. Click the check mark next to a file or folder's name to select it.	1. Click the check mark next to a file or folder's name to select it.
	2. Click the Share button.	2. Click the Share button.
	3. Click Send Email.	3. Click Get a Link.
	4. In the To box, type the e-mail address of the recipient.	4. Click the Create button in either the View Only or View and Edit section.
	5. Type a personal message (optional).	Or
	6. Mark or clear the Recipients Can Edit check box as desired.	Click the Make Public button.
	7. Mark or clear the Require Everyone Who Accesses This to Sign In check box as desired.	5. Press Ctrl+C to copy the code.
		6. Click Done.
	Note: If you mark the check box in Step 7, only people with a Windows account will have access.	7. Click in the application in which you want to share the link, and press Ctrl+V to paste it there.
	8. Click Share.	

Interface Type	Sharing via E-Mail	Getting a Share Link
SkyDrive for Windows	1. In File Explorer (Windows Explorer), right-click the file or folder you want to share, point to SkyDrive, and click Share. The web interface opens. 2. In the preceding steps for "Web interface," go to Step 3.	1. In File Explorer (Windows Explorer), right-click the file or folder you want to share, point to SkyDrive, and click Share. The web interface opens. 2. In the preceding steps for "Web interface," go to Step 3.
Word 2013	1. Choose File⇨Open. 2. Click Browse. 3. Right-click the file or folder on your SkyDrive that you want to share, point to SkyDrive, and click Share. The web interface opens. 4. In the preceding steps for "Web interface," go to Step 3.	1. Choose File⇨Open. 2. Click Browse. 3. Right-click the file or folder on your SkyDrive that you want to share, point to SkyDrive, and click Share. The web interface opens. 4. In the preceding steps for "Web interface," go to Step 3.
Windows 8 SkyDrive app	Not applicable; you can't share files or folders in this app.	Not applicable; you can't share files or folders in this app.

Index

Word 2013 eLearning Kit For Dummies

• *G* •

About the Author

Lois Lowe, MA, is a Microsoft Office Master Instructor and the author of more than 100 books on computer hardware and software, including the *PowerPoint 2013 Bible* and *Excel 2013 eLearning Kit For Dummies*. She is an adjunct instructor of Computer Information Technology at Purdue University, and her corporate training courses online have reached more than one-quarter of a million students for clients such as Hewlett-Packard, Sony, and CNET.

Dedication

To Margaret

Author's Acknowledgments

Thanks to the wonderful editorial staff at John Wiley & Sons, Inc. for another job well done. You guys are top notch!

Publisher's Acknowledgments

Senior Acquisitions Editor: Katie Mohr

Senior Project Editor: Rebecca Huehls

Copy Editor: Amanda Graham

Technical Editor: Sharon Mealka

Editorial Assistant: Annie Sullivan

Sr. Editorial Assistant: Cherie Case

Project Coordinator: Melissa Cossell

Cover Image: ©iStockphoto.com/GlobalStock

Apple & Mac

iPad For Dummies,
6th Edition
978-1-118-72306-7

iPhone For Dummies,
7th Edition
978-1-118-69083-3

Macs All-in-One
For Dummies, 4th Edition
978-1-118-82210-4

OS X Mavericks
For Dummies
978-1-118-69188-5

Blogging & Social Media

Facebook For Dummies,
5th Edition
978-1-118-63312-0

Social Media Engagement
For Dummies
978-1-118-53019-1

WordPress For Dummies,
6th Edition
978-1-118-79161-5

Business

Stock Investing
For Dummies, 4th Edition
978-1-118-37678-2

Investing For Dummies,
6th Edition
978-0-470-90545-6

Personal Finance
For Dummies, 7th Edition
978-1-118-11785-9

QuickBooks 2014
For Dummies
978-1-118-72005-9

Small Business Marketing
Kit For Dummies,
3rd Edition
978-1-118-31183-7

Careers

Job Interviews
For Dummies, 4th Edition
978-1-118-11290-8

Job Searching with Social
Media For Dummies,
2nd Edition
978-1-118-67856-5

Personal Branding
For Dummies
978-1-118-11792-7

Resumes For Dummies,
6th Edition
978-0-470-87361-8

Starting an Etsy Business
For Dummies, 2nd Edition
978-1-118-59024-9

Diet & Nutrition

Belly Fat Diet For Dummies
978-1-118-34585-6

Mediterranean Diet
For Dummies
978-1-118-71525-3

Nutrition For Dummies,
5th Edition
978-0-470-93231-5

Digital Photography

Digital SLR Photography
All-in-One For Dummies,
2nd Edition
978-1-118-59082-9

Digital SLR Video &
Filmmaking For Dummies
978-1-118-36598-4

Photoshop Elements 12
For Dummies
978-1-118-72714-0

Gardening

Herb Gardening
For Dummies, 2nd Edition
978-0-470-61778-6

Gardening with Free-Range
Chickens For Dummies
978-1-118-54754-0

Health

Boosting Your Immunity
For Dummies
978-1-118-40200-9

Diabetes For Dummies,
4th Edition
978-1-118-29447-5

Living Paleo For Dummies
978-1-118-29405-5

Big Data

Big Data For Dummies
978-1-118-50422-2

Data Visualization
For Dummies
978-1-118-50289-1

Hadoop For Dummies
978-1-118-60755-8

Language &
Foreign Language

500 Spanish Verbs
For Dummies
978-1-118-02382-2

English Grammar
For Dummies, 2nd Edition
978-0-470-54664-2

French All-in-One
For Dummies
978-1-118-22815-9

German Essentials
For Dummies
978-1-118-18422-6

Italian For Dummies,
2nd Edition
978-1-118-00465-4

Available in print and e-book formats.

Available wherever books are sold. **For more information or to order direct visit www.dummies.com**

Math & Science

Algebra I For Dummies,
2nd Edition
978-0-470-55964-2

Anatomy and Physiology
For Dummies, 2nd Edition
978-0-470-92326-9

Astronomy For Dummies,
3rd Edition
978-1-118-37697-3

Biology For Dummies,
2nd Edition
978-0-470-59875-7

Chemistry For Dummies,
2nd Edition
978-1-118-00730-3

1001 Algebra II Practice
Problems For Dummies
978-1-118-44662-1

Microsoft Office

Excel 2013 For Dummies
978-1-118-51012-4

Office 2013 All-in-One
For Dummies
978-1-118-51636-2

PowerPoint 2013
For Dummies
978-1-118-50253-2

Word 2013 For Dummies
978-1-118-49123-2

Music

Blues Harmonica
For Dummies
978-1-118-25269-7

Guitar For Dummies,
3rd Edition
978-1-118-11554-1

iPod & iTunes
For Dummies, 10th Edition
978-1-118-50864-0

Programming

Beginning Programming
with C For Dummies
978-1-118-73763-7

Excel VBA Programming
For Dummies, 3rd Edition
978-1-118-49037-2

Java For Dummies,
6th Edition
978-1-118-40780-6

Religion & Inspiration

The Bible For Dummies
978-0-7645-5296-0

Buddhism For Dummies,
2nd Edition
978-1-118-02379-2

Catholicism For Dummies,
2nd Edition
978-1-118-07778-8

Self-Help & Relationships

Beating Sugar Addiction
For Dummies
978-1-118-54645-1

Meditation For Dummies,
3rd Edition
978-1-118-29144-3

Seniors

Laptops For Seniors
For Dummies, 3rd Edition
978-1-118-71105-7

Computers For Seniors
For Dummies, 3rd Edition
978-1-118-11553-4

iPad For Seniors
For Dummies, 6th Edition
978-1-118-72826-0

Social Security
For Dummies
978-1-118-20573-0

Smartphones & Tablets

Android Phones
For Dummies, 2nd Edition
978-1-118-72030-1

Nexus Tablets
For Dummies
978-1-118-77243-0

Samsung Galaxy S 4
For Dummies
978-1-118-64222-1

Samsung Galaxy Tabs
For Dummies
978-1-118-77294-2

Test Prep

ACT For Dummies,
5th Edition
978-1-118-01259-8

ASVAB For Dummies,
3rd Edition
978-0-470-63760-9

GRE For Dummies,
7th Edition
978-0-470-88921-3

Officer Candidate Tests
For Dummies
978-0-470-59876-4

Physician's Assistant Exam
For Dummies
978-1-118-11556-5

Series 7 Exam For Dummie
978-0-470-09932-2

Windows 8

Windows 8.1 All-in-One
For Dummies
978-1-118-82087-2

Windows 8.1 For Dummies
978-1-118-82121-3

Windows 8.1 For Dummies
Book + DVD Bundle
978-1-118-82107-7

e **Available in print and e-book formats.**

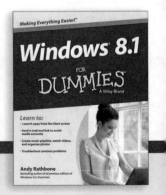

Available wherever books are sold. **For more information or to order direct visit www.dummies.com**

Take Dummies with you everywhere you go!

Whether you are excited about e-books, want more from the web, must have your mobile apps, or are swept up in social media, Dummies makes everything easier.

For Dummies is the global leader in the reference category and one of the most trusted and highly regarded brands in the world. No longer just focused on books, customers now have access to the For Dummies content they need in the format they want. Let us help you develop a solution that will fit your brand and help you connect with your customers.

Advertising & Sponsorships

Connect with an engaged audience on a powerful multimedia site, and position your message alongside expert how-to content.

Targeted ads • Video • Email marketing • Microsites • Sweepstakes sponsorship

21 Million Monthly Page Views & 13 Million Unique Visitors

Custom Publishing

Reach a global audience in any language by creating a solution that will
differentiate you from competitors, amplify your message,
and encourage customers to make a buying decision.

Apps • Books • eBooks • Video • Audio • Webinars

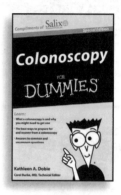

Brand Licensing & Content

Leverage the strength of the world's most popular reference brand to reach
new audiences and channels of distribution.

For more information, visit www.Dummies.com/biz

Dummies products make life easier!

- DIY
- Consumer Electronics
- Crafts
- Software
- Cookware
- Hobbies
- Videos
- Music
- Games
- and More!

For more information, go to **Dummies.com** and search the store by category.

FOR
DUMMIES
A Wiley Brand